Religious Mourning

Religious Mourning

Reversals and Restorations in Psychological Portraits of Religious Leaders

NATHAN CARLIN

WIPF & STOCK · Eugene, Oregon

RELIGIOUS MOURNING
Reversals and Restorations in Psychological Portraits of Religious Leaders

Wipf and Stock
An Imprint of Wipf and Stock Publishers
199 W. 8th Ave., Suite 3
Eugene, OR 97401

www.wipfandstock.com

ISBN 13: 978-1-62032-648-0

Manufactured in the U.S.A. 04/14/2014

For Robert Dykstra

For with much wisdom comes much sorrow;
the more knowledge, the more grief.

—Ecclesiastes 1:18, NIV

Contents

Illustration

Preface

"I went to the *Physicians' Desk Reference*," Princeton Theological Seminary's Robert Dykstra writes, "looked up Dapsone, and there it was—the primary drug used to treat Hansen's Disease, a contemporary (though not the biblical) form of leprosy."[1] He continues: "Though I had suspected it since early childhood, at twenty-seven a doctor confirmed that I was indeed a leper."[2] Dykstra has spent a great deal of his professional life reading, thinking, writing, teaching, and preaching about issues related to the body, such as sexuality. And his academic work cannot be separated from his personal experience, such as his leprosy. There is, in other words, a deep and personal connection for Dykstra between his personal experience and his public scholarship as a pastoral theologian. Indeed, if as a child he experienced his body and sexuality as theologically impure (because, in addition to his medical condition, anti-body and anti-sexuality messages were mediated to him via his religious heritage), as an adult he has more or less come to advocate the reverse upon recognizing and proclaiming "a God who was as concerned with my body as with my soul."[3] With the tools of psychology, Dykstra has been able to create a theology that is healing and restorative in terms of thinking pastorally about the body. This book is about how scholarship, like Dykstra's writings in pastoral theology, heals.

But this book is also about, though less centrally, how scholarship hurts. As scholars, we study things that we are interested in, things that we love. And as scholars we study what we love *critically*. Sometimes this is a painful process, particularly when our methods and methodologies lead us to discover troubling and problematic aspects of the objects of our study. When, for example, the object of study is one's own religion and one

1. Dykstra, Cole Jr., and Capps, *Losers, Loners, and Rebels*, 66.

2. Ibid.

3. Ibid., 67.

uncovers structural problems with one's own tradition that lead to human suffering, the theologian—especially the pastoral theologian—has the responsibility of revising and correcting the tradition as a modern day prophet or reformer by means of their scholarship. I argue that such scholarship is often an act of mourning and that this mourning can be characterized by what I am calling *reversals* and *restorations*. While I do not claim that mourning is the only way one can understand this relationship—one might also speak of joy or transformation—I *do* claim that (1) psychological critiques of religion, such as Sigmund Freud's *The Future of an Illusion*,[4] offer some of the most challenging critiques of religion (which is perhaps why various studies have found that psychologists, more so than other scientists, find it difficult to hold religious beliefs[5]); and (2) religious intellectuals who study religion from a psychological perspective often experience crises of faith[6]—that is, they lose parts of their faith—so it therefore makes sense to explore such loss under the rubric of mourning when thinking about the life and work of those who study some version of religion and psychology. "For with much wisdom comes much sorrow," the writer of Ecclesiastes observes, "the more knowledge, the more grief" (Ecclesiastes 1:18, NIV). I suggest that this poetic verse captures the experience of many scholars who study religion from a psychological perspective; it certainly captures mine. It is my hope that this book, written for students and scholars of psychology of religion and pastoral theology, will offer some healing to those who need it.

4. Freud, *The Future of an Illusion*.

5. Wulff, *Psychology of Religion*, 209–210. Also see Power, *Adieu to God*; Malony, *Psychology and Faith*.

6. Bingaman, *Freud and Faith*.

Acknowledgments

I would like to thank the editorial staff at Wipf and Stock, especially Christian Amondson, acquisitions editor, Matt Wimer, assistant managing editor, and K. C. Hanson, editor-in-chief. I also would like to thank Angela Polczynski for copy-editing this book, and Ian Creeger for type-setting it.

I have benefited from having conversations with many persons about this book. This project began as my dissertation at Rice University, which I wrote during the 2008–2009 academic year. So I would like to thank my dissertation committee, especially William Parsons, for their feedback on this project. Other members included: Jeffrey Kripal, Carol Quillen, Allan Hugh Cole Jr., and Thomas Cole. Thomas Cole, now my colleague at the McGovern Center for Humanities and Ethics, has continued to help me refine my thinking and writing, mentoring me with wisdom and kindness as our friendship has grown over the past decade. Donald Capps read portions of this manuscript many times, and Capps, more than anyone, has shaped my formation as a scholar (and, to a great extent, my formation as a person)—he has been and continues to be a reliable guide, faithful companion, and special friend. I would like to thank Lewis Rambo for his friendship over the years, and for encouraging me to transform my dissertation into a book.

I would like to thank the family members of the subjects of this book: Carolyn Dittes, Nancy Dittes, Anne Hebert Smith, Beverly Bouwsma, and Sarah Bouwsma. Donald Capps and James Dittes also shared stories from their lives with me. This book is much richer for their personal stories. I am grateful for their permission to use their testimonies in this book.

I dedicate this book to Robert Dykstra. Dykstra preached the sermon on the occasion of my ordination as a Minister of Word and Sacrament in the Presbyterian Church (USA) at St. Philip Presbyterian Church (USA) in Houston, Texas, on August 18, 2013, and in the sermon, titled "Zombie

Alleluias," he challenged me to fight the zombies of our day: fundamentalists of all varieties. Can we fight fundamentalism without becoming fundamentalists ourselves, Dykstra asked, following psychoanalyst Adam Phillips? I hope the answer to this question is "yes," but I am not sure. If so, my intuition suggests that mourning would be central to such an endeavor. In any case, I think we—Dykstra and I—are both fundamentalists when it comes to our friendship with one another, and so I dedicate this book to him.

Introduction

> [B]eliefs, disbeliefs, and unbelief reflect something about the nature of psychodynamic object relations and interpersonal experiences.[1]
>
> —Paul Pruyser

MICHELANGELO'S MOSES

Sigmund Freud wrote "The Moses of Michelangelo" anonymously in 1913 (and published it in 1914), but he was not recognized as its author until 1924.[2] In it, Freud discusses the marble statue of Moses sculpted by Michelangelo between 1512 and 1516, and describes the statue in this way:

> The Moses of Michelangelo is represented as seated; his body faces forward, his head with its mighty beard looks to the left, his right foot rests on the ground and his left leg is raised so that only the toes touch the ground. His right arm links the [t]ables of the [l]aw with a portion of his beard; his left arm lies in his lap.[3]

Freud adds that Moses's face seems to display a mixture of "wrath," "pain," and "contempt." He also points out that this sculpture has been interpreted in many various and contradictory ways, which leads him to ask: "Has then the master-hand indeed traced such a vague or ambiguous script in the stone, that so many different readings of it are possible?"[4]

1. Pruyser, *Between Belief and Unbelief*, xiii.
2. Freud, "Moses." The following discussion is a paraphrase of this essay.
3. Ibid., 214.
4. Ibid., 215.

As Freud grapples with the problem of multiple interpretations, he becomes interested in the question as to whether Michelangelo's depiction of Moses is meant to convey the *basic character* of Moses or simply one *particular mood* at a moment in time. He notes that most commentators think that the sculpture conveys one particular mood. The scene is believed to be the descent of Moses from Mount Sinai, with Michelangelo depicting Moses just before he is about to scold his followers for making a golden calf (Exodus 32:19). On this reading, Moses is on the verge of rising to his feet in order to let his rage out on his people. However, following art critic Henry Thode, Freud does not see this as the most viable interpretation, as Thode suggests that Moses is seated (*not* about to spring up) and that the sculpture seems to be a study of character, not mood. Why? First, the tables appear to be firmly lodged and not slipping (most critics have suggested the opposite); and, second, this statue was sculpted for decoration around the base of a tomb for a pope, so it seems unlikely that a fleeting mood would be represented for such a purpose.

Freud next turns to the resources of psychoanalysis to add to Thode's observations. He focuses on two overlooked details in particular: (1) the right hand; and (2) the position of the tables of the law. Freud writes:

> [T]he thumb of the hand is concealed and the index finger alone is in effective contact with the beard. It is pressed so deeply against the soft masses of hair that they bulge out beyond it both above and below, that is, both towards the head and towards the abdomen. The other three fingers are propped upon the wall of his chest and are bent at the upper joints; they are barely touched by the extreme right-hand lock of the beard which falls past them. They have, as it were, withdrawn from the beard. It is therefore not correct to say that the right hand is playing with the beard or plunged in it; the simple truth is that the index finger is laid over part of the beard and makes a deep trough in it. It cannot be denied that to press one's beard with one finger is an extraordinary gesture and one not easy to understand.[5]

Freud continues, "If the *left* side of Moses'[s] beard lies under the pressure of his *right* finger, we may perhaps take this pose as the last stage of some connection between his right hand and the left half of his beard, a connection which was a much more intimate one at some moment before that chosen for representation."[6]

5. Ibid., 222–223.

6. Ibid., 224.

Figure 1: The *Moses* of Michelangelo

On the basis of this interpretation, Freud constructs the following scenario:

1. Moses was sitting calmly.
2. He was disturbed by some noise, and turned his head in the direction of the noise.
3. Moses saw his followers worshiping the golden calf.
4. He became enraged and gripped his beard with contempt.
5. But Moses let go of his anger (and his beard), thus giving us the scene depicted in the statue: Moses's hand is retreating from his beard, with the tablets tucked under his arms.

While most commentators have suggested that Moses is about to stand up and rise in anger, Freud is suggesting the reverse—namely, that Moses is retreating and letting go of his anger.

As noted, Freud also focuses on the positioning of the tables of the law. He suggests that this detail also supports the above scenario in that the reason that Moses's right hand was retreating from his beard was to prevent the tables from falling. So while most critics suggest that Moses is about to smash the tables, Freud argues that Moses is *saving* them. Freud realizes that his interpretation of Michelangelo's artistic representation of Moses is not the Moses of the Bible, because, in the Bible, Moses *did* in fact give into his rage:

> And it came to pass, as soon as he came nigh unto the camp, that he saw the calf, and the dancing: and Moses's anger waxed hot, and he cast the tables out of his hands, and brake them beneath the mount. And he took the calf which they had made, and burnt it in the fire, and ground it to powder, and strawed it upon the water, and made the children of Israel drink of it (Exodus 32:19–20, KJV).[7]

Freud adds: "Michelangelo has placed a different Moses on the tomb of the Pope, *one superior to the historical or traditional Moses*."[8] Why is Michelangelo's *Moses* superior to the Moses of the Bible? Freud suggests that this is so because the *Moses* of Michelangelo depicts "the highest mental achievement that is possible in a man, that of struggling successfully against an inward passion for the sake of a cause to which he has devoted himself."[9] Commenting on this essay, and on this line in particular, Peter Homans notes the view that Freud identified with Moses and, to Freud, Moses's unfaithful followers represented the defections of Alfred Adler and Carl G. Jung (two of Freud's most gifted pupils) from the psychoanalytic movement. Homans also suggests that the tables of the law symbolized, for Freud, the laws of psychoanalysis.[10] And so not only did Freud's interpretation of Michelangelo's *Moses* constitute a reversal of a biblical story of Moses, it also seemed to hold a personal moral meaning for Freud: Freud, following the example of Moses, would contain his own anger toward his unfaithful pupils (Adler and Jung). That is, interpreting Michelangelo's *Moses* helped Freud to struggle against an inward passion (anger) for the sake of a cause to which he had devoted himself (psychoanalysis). This, I suggest, constitutes a kind of religious restoration of Moses for Freud in that Freud, who

7. For an argument for the use of the King James translation of the Bible, see Capps and Carlin, "The Homosexual Tendencies of King James."

8. Freud, "Moses," 233, my emphasis.

9. Ibid.

10. Homans, *Jung*, 112.

self-identified as an atheist,[11] was able to restore part of his Jewish heritage by embracing an artistic portrait of Moses that was both the reverse of the biblical portrait of Moses and congruent with the ideals of psychoanalysis. Freud, who is well-known for writing against religion, nevertheless could not ignore it; it seems he had to engage it.

LOCATING THIS PROJECT

This book, following the spirit of Freud's interpretation of Michelangelo's *Moses*, focuses on the themes of reversals and restorations in three scholarly portraits of religious leaders: Jesus of Nazareth, Augustine of Hippo, and John Calvin. And just as Freud's personal experiences can be seen to have influenced his interpretation of the *Moses* of Michelangelo, I explore how the personal experiences of scholars of religion influence their portraits of religious leaders. This basic project—exploring how a scholar's personal experience influences his or her work—is not new. But what *is* new is that I am using a recent psychological hermeneutic to do so: the mourning religion thesis.[12]

In this book, I advance two basic arguments: (1) scholars who approach religion from a psychological perspective often use psychological methods to critique (reverse) and then to rebuild (restore) religion in a way that is personally meaningful to them; and (2) the relationship between life and work here can be understood in light of the mourning religion thesis. To make my case, I provide three case studies where I explore three recent psychological portraits of religious leaders—Donald Capps's portrait of Jesus,[13] James Dittes's portrait of Augustine,[14] and William Bouwsma's portrait of Calvin[15]—in light of each author's own personal experiences. The upshot of my study is that, while the psychological study of religion is often critical of religion, it also yields its own kind of religiosity, albeit one that is sometimes considered heterodox or even heretical by persons and communities of faith.

11. Gay, *Godless Jew*. For two insightful studies of Freud's "religiosity," see Bakan, *Sigmund Freud* and Parsons, *The Enigma*.

12. Parsons, Jonte-Pace, and Henking, *Mourning Religion*, 1–9.

13. Capps, *Jesus*.

14. Dittes, "Augustine"; Dittes, "Continuities."

15. Bouwsma, *John Calvin*.

This project also builds on the work of Oskar Pfister, the Swiss pastor and longtime friend of Sigmund Freud. In *Christianity and Fear*, Pfister read the history of the church through the lens of psychology and showed how Christianity ceased to be "a religion of love" but became instead "a religion of fear."[16] He surveyed the dynamics of fear from Jesus to Neo-Protestantism, giving psychological attention to major figures along the way, such as the apostle Paul, Martin Luther, and John Calvin, and he sought the use of psychology (particularly Freud's psychoanalysis) to restore to Christianity what he identified as its lost element: love. His project, then, was thoroughly one of reversals and restorations—and so, too, is this one.

THE ORGANIZATION OF THIS BOOK

This book consists of an introduction, a conclusion, and four chapters in between. In chapter 1, I outline the mourning religion thesis and trace its development—this chapter provides the psychological lens through which the following case studies will be read. In chapter 2, I argue that Capps's portrait of Jesus represents a key moment for the overcoming of his own melancholia that enabled him to create a new religious typology of and for men, and that this creativity in Capps can be understood in terms of the mourning religion thesis in the way that Homans presented the theory. In chapter 3, I note that, while Dittes's psychological portrait is indeed deeply influenced by his personal experience—and intentionally so—and while it is also clear that Dittes is doing what he calls "grief work" in his academic work, the mourning religion thesis applies differently to Dittes than it does to Capps. For this reason I draw upon Bertram Cohler's modification of the mourning religion thesis, particularly Cohler's notion of "adaptive melancholia,"[17] and I argue that religion was both the source of and the solution to Dittes's central experience of religious loss. In chapter 4, which focuses on Bouwsma, I argue all three stages of the mourning religion thesis occurred at once in a mixed way while Bouwsma was writing his book on Calvin. Bouwsma, who never had the relationship with his father that he craved, individuated from his father's Dutch Calvinism by writing his book on Calvin, a project he undertook after the death of his father, and, in doing so, he forged his own spirituality by recovering a historical Calvin that was useable for him. In the conclusion, I offer some generalizations about

16. Pfister, *Christianity and Fear*, 24.

17. Cohler, "Nostalgia."

certain strands of pastoral theology and psychology of religion. These strands are often introspective and influenced by psychoanalysis. They also routinely take a subversive stance toward traditional religion[18] but, at the same time, offer new ways in which to understand and to find meaning in religion, much like Freud did when he interpreted Michelangelo's *Moses*.

18. See Myers-Shirk, *Helping the Good Shepherd*, 206–233; and Powlison, *The Biblical Counseling Movement*.

1

The Mourning Religion Thesis

> The defining intuition of pastoral psychology and much of clinical work generally—that participation affects reflection and that the activity of reflection always resists simple discrimination into theological or psychological form—can be carried forward still further, to apply to problems which, though not doctrinal in themselves, are nevertheless germane to theological thought.[1]
>
> —Peter Homans

THE DEVELOPMENT OF THE MOURNING RELIGION THESIS

This chapter focuses on the development of the mourning religion thesis, which was developed over several decades by Peter Homans and his students, primarily in four books: *Jung in Context*,[2] *The Ability to Mourn*,[3] *Symbolic Loss*,[4] and *Mourning Religion*.[5] This chapter provides brief overviews of these four works as well as an interview with Homans. It should be noted at the outset that the mourning religion thesis goes by different

1. Homans, *The Dialogue between Theology and Psychology*, 7.
2. Homans, *Jung*.
3. Homans, *Ability*.
4. Homans, *Symbolic Loss*.
5. Parsons, Jonte-Pace, Henking, *Mourning Religion*.

names (sometimes it is called "the mourning thesis,"[6] and other times it is referred to as "symbolic loss"[7]) and that what I am calling the mourning religion thesis has received a considerable amount of scholarly attention. Indeed, the edited volume *Mourning Religion*, for instance, was the focus of a special session of the 2008 national meeting of the American Academy of Religion as well as a book forum in the journal *Pastoral Psychology* in June 2010.[8] The mourning religion thesis continues to be developed, debated, modified, and applied in ongoing ways.[9]

Jung in Context

As noted, Homans and his students developed the mourning religion thesis over the course of several decades. In 1979, Homans put forward an essential component of the thesis in *Jung in Context: Modernity and the Making of a Psychology* in which he argued for a "contextual" approach—that is, an integration of micro (psychological and biographical) and macro (sociological and anthropological) methods—for understanding the development of psychological systems and theories on the grounds that the then current literature on the origins of psychology tended to focus on the social factors (a sociology of knowledge approach) at the expense of individual insights (a history of ideas approach), and vice versa. He also argued that both approaches tend to ignore the role of religion as a generative force in the formation of psychological ideas.[10] His working hypothesis was that the great and innovative psychologists created their theories as a response to both their social conditions and their intellectual heritage.[11] So in *Jung in Context*, as the title implies, Homans focuses on Carl G. Jung as a great and innovative psychologist and offers a contextual analysis of the formation of Jung's psychology, meaning that he explores Jung's psychology in light of Jung's personal experience, social context, and religious heritage. Loss—both personal and social—is a major theme in Homans's analysis, but he emphasizes context more than loss or mourning in this book.

6. Parsons, "Mourning and Method," 65.

7. Homans, "Symbolic Loss and the Re-Creation of Meaning," 13.

8. Carlin, "Introduction," 345.

9. The thesis has been applied to the Park51 controversy in New York. See Carlin and Khan, "Mourning, Memorials, and Religion."

10. Homans, *Jung*, 1–22, especially 16.

11. Ibid., 7.

The Ability to Mourn

In 1989, Homans *did* emphasize the themes of loss and mourning in *The Ability to Mourn: Disillusionment and the Social Origins of Psychoanalysis.*[12] In this collection of essays, Homans argues that the birth of psychoanalysis was a creative response to the loss of religious and symbolic, especially Judeo-Christian, meanings in western culture. He makes his case by engaging three bodies of literature: scholarship on the origins of psychoanalysis; writings in applied psychoanalysis; and cultural criticism of psychoanalysis. Along the way, he supports his insights by offering case studies that are psychological and sociological in nature. Thus, *The Ability to Mourn* offers a contextual approach as articulated in *Jung in Context.* But *The Ability to Mourn* goes beyond *Jung in Context* by offering a theory of creativity that is understood as a form of mourning.

What is the relationship between mourning and creativity? "The creation of anything new and valuable," Homans argues, "has its origins in the old and in the particular ways the old is abandoned and then altered."[13] Homans offers a three-fold process to explain the relationship between mourning and creativity: when persons and groups experience disillusionment and loss with regard to some cherished object[14] (step one), they then individuate from the loss (step two) and construct some kind of creative response to come to terms with the loss (step three). Psychoanalysis, as a creative response to the de-idealization of religion in western culture (secularization[15]), is a case in point for Homans, which is why, he suggests, that some feel as though psychoanalysis is a "secular religion."[16]

The term "de-idealization" is key for Homans. He notes that several other words have similar meanings, such as disappointment, disillusionment, deploring, renunciation, and disenchantment. What is common to

12. Homans, *Ability.*

13. Ibid., 4.

14. Homans means "object" in a psychoanalytic sense. The *Dictionary of Psychology* defines object in psychoanalytic thought as: "a person, a part of a person, or a symbol representative of either, toward which behaviors, thoughts and desires are oriented. In the classical model, an object is required for one to obtain satisfaction of instincts." See Reber, *Dictionary*, 503–504.

15. For various meanings of secularization, see Taylor, *A Secular Age.* For an interesting psychoanalytic and interpretive social scientific take on the theological significance of secularization, see Fenn, *Time Exposure.* For an insightful, lucid, and brief discussion of the problem of defining secularization, see Shiner, "The Concept of Secularization."

16. Homans, *Ability*, 4.

all of these experiences, he also notes, is object loss. Homans goes on to describe de-idealization in this way:

> It begins with conscious and unconscious idealizations and an enhanced sense of self-esteem, accompanied by feelings of loyalty, merger, and fusion with other objects—persons, ideas, ideals, groups, [and] even a social and intellectual tradition. Since history rarely optimally facilitates psychological development, such mergers are eventually challenged by interpersonal, social, and historical circumstances. As a result, the idealizations lose their firmness and may even crumble, leading to a weakened sense of self, a sense of betrayal, a conviction that important value has been lost, moments of rage at the object (subsequently perceived as having failed the self in some way or other), and a consequent general sense of inner disorganization and paralysis.[17]

"The final disposition of the de-idealization experience," Homans continues, "usually takes one of three directions: (1) it may move toward new knowledge of self, new ideals, and consequent new ideas, or (2) the paralysis can persist, leading to apathy, cynicism, and chronic discontent, or (3) one may disavow the experience entirely and instead attack, often fiercely and rebelliously, the events or persons producing the de-idealization."[18] Homans further suggests that any particular outcome is likely to be a mixture of all three. This is one of Homans's first articulations of the mourning religion thesis.

It should be noted that a number of psychological and sociological thinkers inform Homans, and that he moves freely from one thinker to the next, taking what is useful to derive his own original insights. An unfortunate result from drawing upon so many thinkers is that his book sometimes seems overly technical as well as somewhat convoluted—as perhaps illustrated by the above quotations. In any case, some of the most important concepts and thinkers for Homans's analysis include Sigmund Freud's work on mourning and melancholia,[19] D. W. Winnicott's notions of transitional objects, transitional space, and disillusionment,[20] Melanie Klein's notions of the depressive-position and pining,[21] Max Weber's notion

17. Ibid., 24.
18. Ibid.
19. Freud, "Mourning and Melancholia."
20. Winnicott, "Transitional Objects."
21. Klein, "A Contribution"; "Mourning."

of disenchantment,[22] and Heinz Kohut's notion of de-idealization and his general theory of narcissism.[23]

An Interview with Peter Homans

In an issue of *Criterion*, a bulletin published by the Divinity School of the University of Chicago, William Parsons, a former graduate student of Homans, interviewed Homans about *The Ability to Mourn*.[24] Parsons began the interview by asking Homans about his reasons for writing the book. Homans stated that writing the book helped him to address several topics that he had been interested in over the years, and that it helped him gain a sense of closure in relationship to them. When he began writing on these issues, he felt as though he knew that religion and psychology were important components of modern life—that somehow they contributed to living well—but he did not quite understand how this was so until he wrote the book. Parsons also asked Homans about the central theme of the book: mourning. Homans noted that he uses the concept of mourning in different ways, sometimes referring to an individual's personal experience (such as when a family member dies) and other times as a social phenomenon (such as when a cultural symbol no longer holds its power). Homans then went on to discuss the thesis of the book. Toward the end of the interview, Parsons asks Homans if the university might be viewed as an "institutionalized place of mourning."[25] Homans replies that he did not write about that point *per se*, but adds that the question is very stimulating. He elaborates: "I think that the profession of religious studies, which has evolved in the last forty or fifty years in America and in American universities primarily, and the new departments in which it is found, is the product, in part, of a bit of mourning and a bit of individuation and a bit of creation of meaning."[26] The situation in which scholars of religion find themselves, Homans observes, is one in which they devote all of their time and energy to studying a tradition that, because they are trained to be "objective" and "scientific," they are not allowed to love in their scholarship. This, as Homans sees it, is an experience of loss on the one hand, but, on the other hand, the very creativity of

22. Weber, *The Protestant Ethic*.

23. Kohut, *The Search*.

24. Parsons, "The Ability to Mourn."

25. Ibid., 5.

26. Ibid. Also see Capps, *Religious Studies*.

their scholarship is a form of mourning. Parsons and others, as we will see, pick up on this point.

Symbolic Loss

About ten years after Homans wrote *The Ability to Mourn*, he published an edited volume, titled *Symbolic Loss: The Ambiguity of Mourning and Memory at Century's End*, that carried the culture and mourning relationship further.[27] In *Jung in Context*, Homans, as noted, made a case for a contextual approach, and in *The Ability to Mourn* he used his contextual method for understanding the origins of psychoanalysis and also introduced mourning as a specific lens for understanding culture. In *Symbolic Loss*, Homans continued to make a case for his contextual method and his rubric of mourning, but here he went beyond his previous work by broadening his scope in that this volume considers the relationship between loss and culture beyond the development of a psychological system or theory.

Symbolic Loss consists of four parts that engage loss and mourning from distinct vantage points. Part one focuses on cultural studies; part two focuses on architecture; part three focuses on history; and part four focuses on psychology. The volume has ten contributors: Paul Anderson, Doris Bergen, Mitchell Breitwieser, Peter Homans, Patrick Hutton, Marie-Claire Lavabre, Peter Shabad, Levi Smith, Julia Stern, and James Young. Homans provides a lengthy introductory essay in this volume. In the essay, he sketches a brief history of mourning practices in western culture and observes that there has been a lot of scholarship on the history of mourning; that mourning practices have taken specific forms in the west; and that these practices have declined with the rise of modernization, industrialization, and secularization.

In reviewing various sociological and anthropological scholarship on mourning,[28] Homans establishes a definition of mourning as opposed to grief: Grief is an emotional response (e.g., sorrow, anger, and confusion) to loss, while mourning is a social practice (e.g., religious ceremonies and public memorials) informed by culture. In other words, grief is a painful personal emotion and mourning is a social rite or ritual that attempts to heal or cure it. Homans also points out that grief and mourning can be understood as a process. There is first attachment, followed by loss, then

27. Homans, *Symbolic Loss.*

28. van Gennep, *The Rites*; Hertz, *Death*; Turner, *The Ritual Process.*

grieving and mourning, and, finally, reattachment.[29] This basic structure of mourning informs Homans's thinking about symbolic loss.

Having provided a working definition of mourning, Homans next turns to the field of history to contextualize his thinking. He draws on the work of Philippe Ariès to make the point that death, in western societies, used to be a public and communal event.[30] Christianity provided the rites in which mourning was to be carried out: Ministers and priests gave individuals instructions on what to do with the body, what clothes they should wear, how they should act, how the community should treat those who are mourning, and how long the mourning process should be. Ministers and priests also provided pastoral care for the bereaved. But the democratic, industrial, and technological revolutions challenged and fragmented the traditional sites of authority—that is, religion lost its cohesive power to bind people together—and therefore how to mourn became less clear. Mourning became less public and communal and more personal and internal. Over the course of the twentieth century, Homans observes, persons began turning to psychologists and psychiatrists instead of ministers and priests in the face of loss. Homans refers to this shift in western societies where religion lost its cohesive power as an example of "symbolic loss." He defines symbolic loss as:

> the loss of an attachment to a political ideology or religious creed, or to some aspect or fragment of one, and to the inner work of coming to terms with this kind of loss. In this sense it resembles mourning. However, in the case of symbolic loss the object that is lost is, ordinarily, sociohistorical, cognitive, and collective. The lost object is a symbol or rather a system of symbols and not a person. And the inner work of coming to terms with the loss of such symbols is by no means always followed by generative or creative repair or recovery, but as often by disillusionment, or disappointment, or despair. Some sort of "resignation," along with some mourning, is the best way to describe the most common form of this kind of "coming to terms with the past."[31]

As mourning has become increasingly privatized, certain forms of scholarly literature, Homans observes, have come to function as personal monuments for individual scholars.

29. Homans, *Symbolic Loss*, 3.

30. Ariès, *The Hour*.

31. Homans, *Symbolic Loss*, 20.

Mourning Religion

In 2008, Homans's students published an edited volume (a festschrift) titled *Mourning Religion*.[32] The book is divided into three parts. Part one is on "Loss and Theory Formation in Religious Studies," part two is on "Mourning the (Dis)Contents of Religion," and part three is on "Mourning Religion in Culture." There are nine contributors to the volume: Celia Brickman, Bertram Cohler, Susan Henking, Peter Homans, Diane Jonte-Pace, Harriet Lutzky, William Parsons, Mary Ellen Ross, and Ernest Wallwork. In the introduction, the editors note that, while there has been a great deal of writing on the theorizing of loss during the twentieth and twenty-first centuries, religion has not often been central in these discussions. This volume places religion at the center of the theorizing of loss. They write:

> It is our thesis that religious studies embodies mourning and expresses the process of creative meaning making, that "the profession of religious studies, which has evolved in the last forty or fifty years primarily in American universities . . . is the product, in part, of a bit of mourning and a bit of individuation and a bit of creation of meaning."[33]

The quotation within the quotation above is taken from the interview that Parsons conducted with Homans. The editors also note: "This volume proceeds from the notion that the study of religion in the academy, in both secular and religiously affiliated universities, represents a socially legitimated, institutionalized forum for the mourning of religion (or the melancholic response to the loss of religion) in contemporary culture."[34]

This volume represents the formalization of the mourning religion thesis. In it, each author offers their own version of what mourning (and melancholia) means, and applies it in their own distinctive way. This means that there is not *a* mourning religion thesis—there are *theses*. Yet there is convergence at the thematic level: All of these authors, in one way or another, are writing about the relationships among religion, loss, and culture. I will offer my own articulation of this thesis. But before I do so, however, I will provide a brief case study that employs the mourning religion thesis that will serve as a model for the following three case studies in this book.

32. Parsons, Jonte-Pace, Henking, *Mourning Religion*.

33. Parsons, Jonte-Pace, Henking, "An Introduction," 3–4.

34. Ibid., 5.

PETER HOMANS'S FINAL ARTICULATION OF THE MOURNING RELIGION THESIS

In "Symbolic Loss and the Re-Creation of Meaning: Freud and Eliade as Culture Makers," a chapter in *Mourning Religion*, Homans elaborates on his earlier work and provides his clearest and most compelling articulation and application of the mourning religion thesis, what, as noted, he refers to as symbolic loss.[35] Homans notes that his research question concerns the relationship between personal experience and theoretical construction, or, more plainly, the relationship between life and work. By "work" he means scholarly activities, such as a scholar's published work. And by "life" he means a scholar's personal experience at both micro (individual) and macro (sociohistorical) levels. As the title of his essay intimates, he explores the relationship between life and work in the lives and works of Sigmund Freud and Mircea Eliade.

It is instructive to read Homans's final articulation of what he means by symbolic loss:

> We may theorize these reflections by saying that symbolic loss is a cluster of closely intertwined experiences which often occur in sequential form: attachment, loss, mourning, the revising of memory, and the re-creation of meaning. Attachment is primary: people do not internalize cultural symbols, as psychoanalysts claimed for many years, nor do people simply believe in cultural symbols, as priests have often said. Rather, people form attachments to their symbols in the same way they form attachments to other people. In much the same way, groups and nations form attachments to symbols. Such symbolic attachments produce a sense of social identity based upon a sense of connectedness or belonging to the social structures and ideals they stand for or re-present. In other words, symbols create and represent cultural integration by grounding persons in a shared understanding of an entire way of life. However, the process of modernization repeatedly disconfirms the authority of these symbols, thereby breaking up attachments to them and to the past they represent. When these symbols "die," experiences of loss ensue and cultural disintegration begins.[36]

Homans continues, "Some creative persons are capable of recognizing this loss for what it is and of letting go of it. Such an experience can in turn

35. Homans, "Symbolic Loss and the Re-Creation of Meaning."

36. Ibid., 18.

generate the discovery of something as yet unseen in the new and emerging situation. In the case of the culture maker, this creative work is the construction of what will later become the work."[37]

An Application of the Mourning Religion Thesis: The Case of Sigmund Freud

Homans cites the case of Freud to demonstrate his theory about symbolic loss and the creation of new meaning. In using Freud as a case study, he explores a number of losses in Freud's life. In 1896, Freud was forty years old. He was married with children and living in Vienna, struggling to get by as a neurologist. He had been thinking about the unconscious on account of his correspondence with a friend, Wilhelm Fleiss, but he probed deeper into the concept after the death of his father, trying to make sense of his own feelings. This loss, Freud later came to see, was what prompted him to write *The Interpretation of Dreams*,[38] and later led him to the view that a man's greatest loss in life is the death of his father.

Another loss that Freud experienced involved his Jewish heritage. When Freud was a boy, Jews were generally tolerated in Vienna. But when Carl Luger, who had run on a platform of anti-Semitism, was elected mayor of Vienna in 1897, Freud, who was committed to tolerance and liberalism, was greatly disillusioned by this turn of events because, as Homans put it, "Luger's election meant that the liberals had abandoned the Jews."[39] Both of these losses—the death of his father and the loss of an ideal (i.e., political liberalism)—led Freud to search inside himself, and what he discovered, Homans argued, was the material for psychoanalysis.

Homans next describes the formation of the psychoanalytic movement. He notes that it first began with a few persons interested in Freud's *The Interpretation of Dreams*. They met weekly, calling themselves the Wednesday Psychological Society, and the circle grew and quickly became a movement. In 1908 Jung joined. Freud and Jung grew very close, exchanging many letters—over 300 in total. Freud now had a gifted young student, and Jung had a mentor. Freud even publically named Jung as his successor to the psychoanalytic movement, not only because Jung was so gifted, but also, and perhaps more importantly, because Jung was a Gentile.

37. Ibid.

38. Freud, *Interpretation of Dreams*.

39. Homans, "Symbolic Loss and the Re-Creation of Meaning," 21.

The success of the psychoanalytic movement, Freud believed, depended on reaching out to the Gentiles in a world that was becoming increasingly hostile to Jews. But the relationship went sour, and Freud and Jung cut off relations around 1912. Homans notes that this loss was devastating to Freud and occasioned the onset of a depression because Freud believed that Jung's departure meant the death of psychoanalysis. But Freud, however, responded in a deeply creative way. He significantly revised his model of the mind and psychosexual development by introducing the concept of narcissism.[40]

After losing Jung, Freud gained a new student, Karl Abraham, with whom he believed he was more compatible because Abraham shared his Jewish heritage. Contrary to Freud's initial fears about losing Jung, the psychoanalytic movement proceeded to gain a new stability. Yet a new problem, or the return of an old problem, began to preoccupy Freud—namely, Freud's relationship with his Jewishness. Here Homans finds another major loss in Freud's life, that is, the loss of his Jewish identity. Homans notes that Freud, in his later years, turned away from clinical writings and shifted to more cultural explorations. In *Moses and Monotheism*,[41] Freud argued that Jews suffer from a collective narcissism that was inculcated in them by Moses with the idea that they are God's "chosen people" (cf. Deuteronomy 7:6). Freud observes that Jews, for religious reasons, believe that they are special and superior to all other races, and he calls on them to disavow this past and to overcome their narcissism by means of psychoanalysis. In turn, Freud simultaneously calls on Gentiles (such as Germans) to disavow their nationalism, their sense that they are superior, so that neither Jewish collective narcissism nor Jewish oppression will exist. "In a basic and general sense," Homans writes, "Freud is here simply re-affirming what he had always thought and said. Psychoanalysis was a science and as such it explained and discredited religion. . . . Where then is the loss?"[42] Homans replies: "The loss is in the risk that Freud took in writing this book. He risked offending fellow Jews whose Jewish identity had a strong grounding in belief, and he risked being criticized by them for his merely social attachment to the Jewish historic community."[43] Further, "he also risked rejection

40. Homans, *Ability*, 18–19; also see Gay, *Freud*, 338.

41. Freud, *Moses and Monotheism*.

42. Homans, "Symbolic Loss and the Re-Creation of Meaning," 25–26.

43. Ibid., 26.

by the scientific and nonreligious community, which might find in his minimally naturalistic faith some sort of crypto-religious commitment."[44]

This final loss that Homans is describing is more difficult to see than the others, which are rather straightforward. Here Homans is saying that the loss is in the writing of *Moses and Monotheism*. If so, what, then, is the creative response if the writing of *Moses and Monotheism* is the loss? It seems that this is a unique case in that *Moses and Monotheism* simultaneously represents a kind of loss as well as a creative response to the loss. In other words, in this particular instance of religious mourning, the loss is *anticipated*, and it is this anticipated loss to which Freud is creatively responding. Given that Freud was a gifted writer, and given that *Moses and Monotheism* is perhaps Freud's most poorly written and convoluted work,[45] perhaps what we have in this final instance is an inability to mourn. While *Moses and Monotheism* (published in 1937) is a much more comprehensive work than "The Moses of Michelangelo" (published in 1914), it is much less convincing, and perhaps this is related in some way to the return of anti-Semitism and the rise of Nazism in Europe, losses that must have been emotionally devastating to Freud. It would have been much harder, it seems to me, for Freud to create new meaning after the onset of World War II than World War I.

CONCLUSION: AN ARTICULATION OF THE MOURNING RELIGION THESIS

To conclude this chapter, I want to articulate a version of the mourning religion thesis; this articulation will inform the rest of the book.[46]

People who study religion professionally are often if not always drawn to the study of religion out of some religious conviction of their own. However, during the course of their study and also by means of some personal life experience of loss that is connected to religion in some way, students of religion become disappointed or disillusioned with religion, and they subsequently mourn religion in various ways, often by means of their scholarship. In other words, such scholars separate or individuate themselves from

44. Ibid.

45. See the editor's note on *Moses and Monotheism*: Freud, *Moses and Monotheism*, 4.

46. The following articulation of the mourning religion thesis has been adapted from Carlin and Khan, "Mourning, Memorials, and Religion." Also see Carlin, "Reversers and Restorers," 408–414.

their religious loss, and they subsequently create new meaning that is often outside of the realm of their former or current religious tradition. The new meaning that they create is usually in the form of articles and books; books and articles become, as it were, personal memorials for individual scholars. For some scholars, reading and writing take the place of fasting and prayer. The mourning religion thesis suggests that these scholars are still religious but in unconventional ways, and thus their work can be viewed as a form of religious mourning.

One way this theory can be tested is by means of case studies. Homans, as noted, has applied the theory to Sigmund Freud, Carl G. Jung, and Max Weber,[47] and Parsons has applied the theory to lesser-known intellectuals.[48] In a review of *Mourning Religion*, Jacob Belzen applauded this idiographic (case study) approach and called for more such studies to further validate the theory.[49] To further test the mourning religion thesis, this book follows the example of Parsons to answer the call of Belzen by focusing on the lives and works of Donald Capps, James Dittes, and William Bouwsma.

47. Homans, *Jung*; Homans, *Ability*; Homans, *Symbolic Loss*.

48. Parsons, "Mourning and Method."

49. Belzen, "Mourning Religion?" Also see Belzen, *Psychology of Religion*.

2

Reframing Religion[1]

> My favorite Bible verse in boyhood was John 14:6: "Jesus said to him, 'I am the way, and the truth, and the life. No one comes to the Father except by me.'" In the course of writing this book [on Jesus], I was mindful of the desire to keep faith with this boy and have done so, I believe, by striving to write a study of Jesus that was not afraid to ask questions in search of a more reliable truth.[2]
>
> —Donald Capps

INTRODUCTION

Donald Eric Capps, William Harte Felmeth Professor of Pastoral Psychology at Princeton Theological Seminary, was born to Holden and Mildred Capps on January 30, 1939. He had three siblings: Walter, Roger, and Douglas. He married Karen Virginia Docken on August 22, 1964, and they had their only child, John Michael Capps, on July 19, 1970. Capps was ordained in the Evangelical Lutheran Church in America on June 5, 1972. He received his BA (he majored in both English and Philosophy) from Lewis and Clark College in 1960; a BD from Yale Divinity School in 1963; a STM

1. This chapter, as with all of the chapters in this book, derives from my dissertation. But I also published this chapter as a journal article in *Pastoral Psychology* (see Carlin, "In Search of a More Reliable Truth"). This chapter draws from both my dissertation and the journal article.

2. Capps, *Jesus*, xiii.

from Yale Divinity School in 1965; a MA from the University of Chicago in 1966; a PhD from the University of Chicago in 1970; and an honorary ThD from the University of Uppsala in 1989. Capps took an Instructor position in the Department of Religious Studies at Oregon State University in the spring and summer of 1969, and he returned to the University of Chicago the following fall to take an Assistant Professor position. He taught there from 1969 to 1974. He then moved to the University of North Carolina at Charlotte, where he taught for two years (1974–1976) as an Associate Professor. Then he took an Associate Professor position at the Graduate Seminary of Phillips University. He taught there from 1976 to 1981, was promoted to Full Professor in 1978, and then moved to Princeton Theological Seminary as a Full Professor in 1981, where he stayed until his retirement in 2009. He continues to teach as Adjunct Professor at Princeton Theological Seminary.[3]

While Capps is one of the most prolific writers in psychology of religion, he made his name in academia in the field of pastoral care and counseling, as most of his monographs were written in this field.[4] Indeed, the title of this chapter—Reframing Religion—is a reference to his *Reframing: A New Method in Pastoral Care*.[5] He also wrote a number of monographs in psychology of religion.[6] While Capps has written dozens of books (over twenty-five monographs, six coauthored books, two edited books, and twelve coedited books) and hundreds of articles,[7] this chapter is primarily concerned with one of his books—namely, *Jesus: A Psychological Biography*.[8] I will, to be sure, draw on his other work as well because they will aid in understanding his psychobiography of Jesus as well as the relationship between his life and work.

There are four basic components of this chapter. In part one, I present Capps's psychological interpretation of Jesus. I present information about Capps's personal life in part two, drawing from various sources, focusing primarily on his childhood and his self-described origins of his religious

3. I obtained this information from Capps's curriculum vitae.

4. See, for example, Capps, *Pastoral Care*; Capps, *Pastoral Care and Preaching*; Capps, *Life Cycle Theory*; Capps, *Giving Counsel*; Capps, *The Poet's Gift*, Capps, *Agents of Hope*; Capps, *Living Stories*; Capps, *Young Clergy*; and Capps, *Fragile Connections*.

5. Capps, *Reframing*.

6. See, for example, Capps, *Men, Religion, and Melancholia*, as well as Capps, *Men and Their Religion*.

7. Dykstra and Cole, "Books and Articles by Donald Capps."

8. Capps, *Jesus*.

life. In part three, I apply the mourning religion thesis to Capps's life and work, demonstrating the importance of his writing *Jesus* for his own transformation of melancholia into mourning. Finally, in part four, I include Capps's reaction to my argument as well as further reflections.

PART ONE: CAPPS'S PSYCHOLOGICAL PORTRAIT OF JESUS

Capps divides *Jesus* into three parts. In part one, which consists of two chapters, Capps engages four contemporary portraits of Jesus written by historical Jesus scholars; this procedure reflects Capps's belief that psychobiographers should build on the work of specialists.[9] Chapter 1 focuses on the work of E. P. Sanders and John P. Meier, and chapter 2 focuses on the work of John Dominic Crossan and Marcus J. Borg. In part two of the book, which consists of three chapters, Capps deals with methodological issues in psychobiography and psychohistory: chapter 3 deals with psychobiography, chapter 4 with psychohistory, and chapter 5 with the social world of Jesus's day. This sets the stage for part three of the book, which constitutes Capps's own psychological portrait of Jesus. In part three, which also consists of three chapters, Capps deals with Jesus's childhood in chapter 6, with Jesus's exorcisms and healings in chapter 7, and with Jesus's personality in chapter 8. This chapter will focus on part three of Capps's book.[10]

Jesus's Childhood

Capps discusses several scholarly reconstructions of Jesus's early childhood and Jesus's relationship with his father Joseph in chapter 6. These topics are barely mentioned in the canonical Gospels; this is why this period in Jesus's life is sometimes referred to as "the hidden years." The statements that Jesus does make about his family (or families in general) sometimes seem odd and confusing, further obfuscating Jesus's childhood. For example, biblical scholars have puzzled over such sayings as this one: "Whoever comes to me and does not hate father and mother, wife and children, brothers and sisters, yes, and even life itself, cannot be my disciple" (Luke 14:26).

9. Ibid., x. For an excellent overview of methodological issues relating to psychobiography, see Schultz, *Handbook of Psychobiography.*

10. For a summary of *Jesus*, written by Capps himself, see Capps, "A Summary of Jesus."

In reconstructing the childhood of Jesus, scholars grapple with the little material that is available, and they often come to very different conclusions. Capps presents several competing conclusions, which will be outlined below.

Jesus's Childhood as Ordinary and Typical

The first view regarding Jesus's early years that Capps discusses is that of John Miller.[11] Capps notes that Miller's reconstruction of Jesus's early childhood is congruent with Meier's[12] (which Capps summarized in part one of *Jesus*) in that they both argue that Jesus's early years were "ordinary" and "typical." But, Capps notes, if Jesus's early years were so ordinary and typical, how then can one account for Jesus's *atypical* behavior as an adult—that is, how did he become such an exceptional man?

Meier and Miller account for Jesus's atypical behavior and exceptional accomplishments by emphasizing his relationship with John the Baptist. They argue that Jesus led an ordinary life until he met John, after which he had a profound religious experience that led him into a life of ministry. Capps points out that any explanation that focuses on Jesus's relationship with John the Baptist needs to deal with three questions: (1) why would Jesus lead a celibate life prior to meeting John (as he seems to have done); (2) why did he experience tensions within his family (as indicted by verses such as Luke 14:26 and John 2:4); and (3) why would he be prompted to follow John in the desert in the first place? Capps thinks that these are clues that Jesus's childhood was not as ordinary and typical as Meier and Miller would have us believe.

Capps notes that Miller deals with these questions by suggesting that Joseph died when Jesus was a teenager. Jesus's otherwise normal and positive experience of childhood was disrupted by the death of his father, and this explains why Jesus apparently did not marry because it would have been Joseph's responsibility to find Jesus a wife. Miller also thinks that Jesus was the firstborn son of Joseph (cf. Luke 2:7), and that, after the death of Joseph, Jesus would have bore the responsibilities of Joseph for the household—this, then, provides insight as to why Jesus would have experienced tensions with his family (i.e., he was forced into a role of responsibility). Jesus's experiences with John the Baptist in the desert provided Jesus with

11. Miller, *Jesus at Thirty*.

12. Meier, *A Marginal Jew*.

a religious justification for leaving his family and procuring his independence, an independence that was threatened on account of his duties as the firstborn son. Capps also points out that a key part of Miller's reconstruction of Jesus's childhood emphasizes the fact that Jesus called God "Abba" (which is an affectionate name for God) and that he thinks that Jesus did so due to his positive experiential relationship with Joseph.

Joseph as Adopting Father

Capps next discusses Jane Schaberg's thesis in *The Illegitimacy of Jesus* that, as her title intimates, Joseph was not the biological father of Jesus (and that some other man was the biological father of Jesus).[13] Capps notes that Schaberg focuses on the implications of this illegitimacy for Mary, and that he draws on her analysis to focus on the implications of this illegitimacy for Jesus. Thus, Schaberg's view is in stark contrast to Miller's argument that the childhood of Jesus was ordinary and typical.

Several aspects of Schaberg's argument are particularly noteworthy. She examines the genealogy of Jesus as reported in the Gospel of Matthew (Matthew 1:1–17), and notes a pattern of A begot B, B begot C, C begot D, and so forth. She observes that this pattern breaks down when it comes to Joseph: "Jacob begot Joseph the husband of Mary; of her was begotten Jesus, called the Christ" (Matthew 1:16). Joseph, according to the genealogy, did not "beget" Jesus. What does this deviation mean? The traditional answer to this deviation is the doctrine of virgin birth—that is, Joseph is not listed as the father because the Holy Spirit is the father of Jesus (cf. Matthew 1:18–20). But Schaberg thinks that such modern readings of these verses are anachronistic and that these texts would have been understood quite differently in their Jewish-Christian context. In Jewish-Christian culture, it was believed that God and human beings worked together to conceive a child, so *all* births in this sense are divine—there is nothing unusual or miraculous, Schaberg argues, about stating that the Holy Spirit is the father of Jesus. But if not a miracle, what then is being communicated by indicating that Joseph is the father (but not the begetter) of Jesus? Schaberg thinks that this verse indicates that Joseph legally adopted Jesus. And so Schaberg paints Joseph as a compassionate man who willingly adopted a boy whom he did not beget because an angel told him to adopt this child (cf. Matthew 1:20–21).

13. Schaberg, *The Illegitimacy of Jesus*.

Capps finds the argument that Jesus was illegitimate compelling. But he finds fault with Schaberg's assumption that Joseph *willingly* adopted Jesus. Capps questions this assumption on the grounds that Schaberg does not consider the fact that the Gospel of Matthew could be constructing an idealized portrait of Joseph, and he wonders, based on distinctions in law between Judea and Galilee, if Joseph proceeded with his marriage plans because "he realized he was trapped, either because he could not prove that he was *not* the child's father or that he did not have the requisite social standing in the community to bring charges that would have been taken seriously."[14] Capps writes: "Whether an angelic voice [cf. Matthew 1:20–21] can put a helpless man's resentment and rage to rest . . . seems doubtful."[15]

Jesus as a Fatherless Son

Citing the work of Andries van Aarde, Capps discusses a third possibility concerning the relationship between Jesus and Joseph: that Jesus was "a fatherless son."[16] Van Aarde's main point is that there is not enough textual evidence to know if Mary was seduced or raped (Schaberg's argument), and that the most solid conclusion, textually speaking, is simply concluding that Joseph, for whatever unknown reason, was absent from Jesus's life. A primary basis for this claim is that Joseph is not mentioned in the earliest sources (i.e., Paul, Mark, Q, and Thomas). More evidence in this regard is that Joseph seems not to have partaken in his expected fatherly duties, such as arranging for Jesus to be married. Van Aarde also explores the literature concerning the rules regarding social status relevant for Jesus's time and place, and he notes that fatherless sons were excluded from the societal structures of honor, such as religious rituals. Jesus therefore would not have been considered to be a part of the Assembly of God's people, and this explains why Jesus would have been attracted to the teachings of John the Baptist. Capps writes: "Through John's baptism, performed at the Jordan river, Jesus could—and did—experience symbolically what he was deprived of literally, which was the status of 'a son of Abraham, son of God.'"[17]

14. Capps, *Jesus*, 145.

15. Ibid., 146.

16. Van Aarde, "Social Identity, Status Envy, and Jesus' *Abba*."

17. Capps, *Jesus*, 150.

Capps's Portrait of the Hidden Years

Capps supports the hypothesis that Jesus was conceived illegitimately by means of rape or seduction (Schaberg), and he also thinks that Jesus was fatherless (van Aarde). But he modifies Schaberg's and van Aarde's views in a significant way: Capps argues that Jesus did live in Joseph's house but that Joseph chose not to adopt Jesus, leaving Jesus both legally and psychologically in need of a father. Capps writes, "If Jesus was viewed as illegitimate by villagers, and was therefore the victim of considerable social ostracism, this would have affected his marriage-ability, his occupational prospects, his chances for an education, and, of course, for participating in the religious life of the community."[18] He continues: "In that case, we would not be surprised if what most scholars believe happened did in fact happen, that is, that he left Nazareth to make his 'home' in Capernaum; that he probably did not marry and father children of his own; that, like other dispossessed sons, he became a *tekton* [a carpenter]; and that he exhibited at least *some* personality characteristics comparable to wandering Cynics."[19]

Capps, then, out of the three scholars discussed here (Miller, Schaberg, and van Aarde), argued for the worst-case scenario in terms of reconstructing Jesus's childhood. Miller argued that Jesus's childhood was ordinary and typical until the death of Joseph; Schaberg argued that Jesus experienced considerable social ostracism on account of his illegitimacy but that Joseph adopted him; van Aarde contended that Jesus was a fatherless son (because Joseph was physically absent); and Capps argued that Jesus was illegitimate and a fatherless son because Joseph, though physically present, would not adopt him. If Capps's portrait is accurate, many of the strange sayings of Jesus—sayings that seem to be anti-family (cf. Matthew 10:37; Thomas 55, 101)—begin to make sense. So, too, does his use of Abba (Mark 14:36) and his concern for children (Matthew 19:14).

Jesus as Village Psychiatrist

In chapter 7 of *Jesus*, Capps offers a psychological explanation to account for how Jesus healed.[20] In short, he argues that Jesus healed diseases and ill-

18. Ibid., 161.

19. Ibid.

20. For an extended discussion of Capps's views on Jesus's work as a healer, see Capps, *Jesus the Village Psychiatrist*.

nesses by addressing their psychological dimension that was in many cases due to anxiety related to sexuality and/or aggression. Capps notes that his argument is a critique of biblical scholars (such as Crossan[21]) who invoke the illness and disease distinction often made by medical anthropologists[22] to argue that Jesus did not heal physical diseases but only addressed social illnesses. Capps argues that diseases are *psycho*biological and that illnesses are *psycho*social—there is a psychological dimension to both—and that Jesus healed both illnesses and diseases by attending to their psychological dimensions.

Capps discusses a number of the exorcisms and healings of Jesus in this chapter. To illustrate how Capps offers his psychological explanations, I will discuss one of them: the case of a demon-possessed boy found in Mark 9:14–29 (cf. Matthew 17:14–18 and Luke 9:37–43). In this story, a man brings his son to Jesus after Jesus's disciples were not able to heal the boy. His father explains to Jesus that his son has a spirit that makes him unable to speak and that sometimes the spirit causes the boy to fall down, grind his teeth, and foam from the mouth. When the boy was brought to Jesus, the boy indeed fell to the ground, convulsed, and foamed from the mouth. Jesus asked the father how long this had been happening. The father said that it has been happening since childhood and that sometimes the spirit had caused the boy to fall into fire as well as water. Jesus instructed the spirit to come out of the boy, and it did, after a fit of crying and convulsing by the boy. The boy subsequently fell limp. The crowd around them thought that the boy had died. But Jesus picked the boy up by the hand, and he was made well. The disciples later asked Jesus why they had not been able to cast out the spirit, and Jesus said that "This kind can come out only through prayer" (Mark 9:29).

Capps begins his discussion of this story by noting that many biblical scholars think that this boy suffered from epilepsy (and that other biblical scholars have suggested the diagnosis of hysteria). He then discusses Ian Hacking's study of the "mad traveler" or "fuguer" phenomenon—a phenomenon where a person would travel a great distance and have no memory of how one got there or how one returned home—in late nineteenth century medical theory, because there was a debate then as to whether such behavior was caused by a form of epilepsy or by hysteria.[23] Based on Hack-

21. Crossan, *Jesus*, 80–82.

22. Kleinman, *Patients and Healers*.

23. Hacking, *Mad Travellers*.

ing's discussion, Capps thinks that it may not be possible to decide which diagnosis is right for the demon-possessed boy in Mark 9:14–29 but that, in any case, psychological factors would still be at work even if this were a case of epilepsy. That is to say, a neurological diagnosis would not preclude psychological factors in the boy's presentation of his symptoms.

What psychological factors might be influencing the boy's presentation of symptoms? Capps thinks that the father's statement that the spirit's intention to destroy the boy is an important clue. Capps suggests that the spirit's intention to destroy the boy is a case of repressed rage that is manifesting itself in self-destructive behavior: "While the unconscious motivation behind such self-destructive acts cannot be explained on the basis of the presented facts, we may surmise . . . that these acts internalize a desire to inflict punishments on someone else, quite possibly his mother."[24] If the boy's expression of symptoms were a reaction to some experience in his childhood, these experiences, Capps further surmises, must have been quite severe in order to cause such serious self-destructive symptoms as falling in water or fire. Capps continues: "If I were to hazard a guess, I would say that the boy's mother beat him unmercifully, as prescribed by Proverbs 23:13: 'Do not withhold discipline from your children; if you beat them with a rod, they will not die,' and Proverbs 29:15, 'The rod and reproof give wisdom, but a mother is disgraced by a neglected child.'"[25] If this were the case, Capps argues, the symptoms would "reflect his internalization of rage against his mother, a rage that he dares not act upon (e.g., by hitting back), but instead acts out in the form of episodes involving falling into fire and water."[26] Capps also points out that the mother is not mentioned in this story and that it is the boy's father who brings him to Jesus. He adds that Meier has observed that Jesus interacts with the father (and not the spirit) in this story, which is unlike other episodes in the Gospels (see, e.g., Luke 8:30–31). And Capps further notes that (1) there seems to have been something at stake for Jesus's own identity in this story, as Jesus rebukes the father for doubting Jesus's ability to heal; and (2) at the end of the story, Jesus explains to the disciples that some kind of spirits can only be cast out by means of prayer, thus intimating that it was Jesus's prayer to Abba that healed the boy. By healing this boy, Capps concludes, Jesus's own sonship—that he (Jesus) was a son of Abba—was also affirmed.

24. Capps, *Jesus*, 174.

25. Ibid., 175.

26. Ibid.

Jesus's Personality

In chapter 8, Capps offers his sketch of the personality of Jesus, and in doing so he focuses on the temple disturbance (Matthew 21:12–17; Mark 11:15–19; Luke 19:45–48; and John 2:13–22). He argues in this chapter that Jesus's personality was "utopian-melancholic." By "utopian" Capps does not mean that Jesus saw himself as a social reformer; he means utopian in more of a psychological (and less of a social or political) sense. Utopia, he argues, meant for Jesus living in a state beyond anxiety. He discusses various theories of utopia and notes that the idea of utopia being located in the future is a rather late development (as utopia literally means "no place") and that this "no place" can be in the here and now just as much as it can be in the future. Capps thinks that Jesus's expression of utopian thinking would have been oriented toward the here and now—and not toward future social reform—because Jesus was, in all likelihood, a peasant, and peasants usually concern themselves with more proximate concerns such as relief from boredom and hunger rather than major social reform.

By using the term "melancholic" Capps is invoking his previous theorizing on male melancholia.[27] His theory is psychoanalytic and is derived from two of Freud's essays,[28] and the key point is that boys develop a melancholy self[29] on account of their emotional separation from their mothers between the ages of three and five and that boys experience this separation as maternal abandonment. Boys, then, develop ambivalent attitudes toward their mothers as well as things and situations that recall their maternal estrangement. In *Jesus*, Capps focuses on Freud's insight that the home (and things related to the home) have strong maternal overtones and associations, and Capps explores various stories and sayings of and about Jesus as reported in the gospels noting that various sayings of Jesus reflect maternal (or home-related) ambivalence, such as Matthew 8:19–20, Mark 3:31–34, Luke 9:58, Luke 11:27–28, Thomas 79, Thomas 86, and Thomas 101. Perhaps one of the most telling is Thomas 101, which serves as an epigram for Capps's chapter: "For my mother gave me falsehood, but my true mother gave me life."[30]

27. Capps, *Men, Religion, and Melancholia.*

28. Freud, "Mourning and Melancholia"; Freud, "The Uncanny."

29. Capps, *At Home in the World*, xiii–xiv.

30. Capps, *Jesus*, 219.

The episode in Jesus's life to which Capps gives the most attention is the disruption in the temple because this episode, Capps argues, illustrates most clearly both Jesus's utopian personality *and* his melancholic personality. He notes that there is widespread agreement among biblical scholars that there is little reason to doubt the historicity of this event, and that the story, as noted, is found in all four of the canonical gospels. And while there are differences in the four accounts (John's account, as is typical of John, is the most divergent), the gist of the story is the same: Jesus and his disciples go into the temple and Jesus becomes enraged with what he sees. Specifically, he is upset that people are selling doves and changing money—he says that they have made this house of worship into a den of thieves—and so he drives out the sellers and the money changers. The religious authorities wanted to kill him for his actions, but a mass of people were captivated by the words of Jesus, and thus these authorities knew that now was not the time that they could kill him.

Capps argues that the disturbance in the temple was an impulsive (spontaneous) act by Jesus on the grounds that Jesus seems to have acted alone and was the only one arrested for the disturbance. This suggests that his actions were not a part of an orchestrated takeover. But what, one may ask, was Jesus trying to accomplish by means of this disturbance? Was he intending to "cleanse" the temple symbolically, or was he intending to "destroy" the temple symbolically? Capps notes that scholars are divided on how to interpret Jesus's actions here, but that the symbolic cleansing view seems to have less historical basis. Capps takes the symbolic destruction view, but also he thinks that Jesus's actions were overdetermined: "[T]he deeper layer of Jesus'[s] action *does* fall under the terms 'cleansing of the temple,' though not in its traditional meaning, that is, as Jesus'[s] objection to fraudulent buying, selling, and money changing operations,"[31] because "[t]he 'cleansing' was much deeper than that, and was therefore on a continuum with Jesus'[s] role as exorcist-healer. This cleansing concerned his illegitimacy, and his mother's role in it. Because of this, it went to the very core of his personal identity conflicts."[32] He goes on:

> Thus, ironically, the temple cleansing tradition, while without historical basis, unintentionally offers a psychoanalytic interpretation of Jesus'[s] action. Besides the tradition that the temple is God's abode on earth, a parallel tradition affirmed that it symbolizes the

31. Ibid., 256.

32. Ibid.

> mother. If the temple belongs to God, the temple itself is maternal. It symbolizes her body. Thus, it may have all the implications of male ambivalence toward it that were brought out in our [previous] discussion.[33]

Capps suggests that what needed cleansing was Jesus's mother's body, because of the illicit sexual act that led to the conception of Jesus: "Through this act, he symbolically 'cleansed' the mother's body of its impurity—restoring her to her virginal innocence—and completed his own transformation from the son of a nameless seducer (a mere 'begetter') to son of 'Abba.'"[34]

Capps's portrait of Jesus can be summarized as follows. Jesus was illegitimately conceived and grew up as a fatherless son because Joseph chose not to adopt him. As a fatherless son, Jesus suffered a considerable amount of social stigma. He was not able to marry, lived as a peasant, and was excluded from the religious social structure. For these reasons, Jesus was attracted to the teachings of John the Baptist, as John's teachings provided a means to God outside of the traditional religious establishment: Jesus became a son of Abba. Jesus's teachings were informed by his own experiences as someone living on the fringes of society, and he thus showed a special consideration for others in similar (i.e., disempowered) situations, such as the poor, the neglected, women, children, and the oppressed. Jesus was able to heal and to exorcise because he was able to address the psychological factors, especially those relating to anxiety, involved in various diseases and illnesses, and his final act of exorcism involved cleansing the temple (and his mother). This act, which directly led to his arrest, was Jesus's final act of triumph, the moment in which he exorcised his own melancholia and experienced the bliss of utopia.

PART TWO: THE CHILDHOOD ROOTS OF CAPPS'S RELIGIOUS LIFE

Having provided a brief summary of key aspects of Capps's psychobiography of Jesus, I now want to turn to a discussion of Capps's personal life (focusing especially on the childhood roots of his religious life) so as to set the stage for understanding his work in light of the mourning religion thesis.

33. Ibid., 257.

34. Ibid., 259.

He has made many self-disclosures in his publications over the years; these self-disclosures will serve as the primary basis for my analysis.

The Child's Song

In 1991, Capps gave the presidential lecture to the Society for the Scientific Study of Religion in Pittsburgh, Pennsylvania. His talk turned out to be quite provocative. It was titled "Religion and Child Abuse: Perfect Together." He subsequently published a book based on this talk, titled *The Child's Song: The Religious Abuse of Children*.[35] In both the talk and the book Capps noted that while many have pointed out that Christianity has encouraged physical child abuse[36] few have given much attention to the fact that Christianity has also fostered a kind of subtle emotional abuse by means of its doctrines, such as notions of an approaching apocalypse, a sadistic hell, the atonement, and the story of the virgin birth.

Given that this book—i.e., my book—is about the relationship between personal experience and public scholarship, one would naturally wonder if Capps were abused as a boy: Is this the reason that he chose to write *The Child's Song*? He makes no such disclosure in his writings to confirm such a hypothesis. But, on the basis of certain self-disclosures in our letters, when I asked Capps if he had experienced his mother as verbally abusive, he replied: "I don't think I would use the words 'verbally abusive' to describe her—the control was more like what [William] Stafford describes in his poems," such as "Vacation Trip," "Vocation," and "Mother's Day." None of these poems depict Stafford's mother in an especially positive light. Capps added:

> I think that I felt she had a way of putting a damper on things when I would have preferred a more positive approach to life. I suppose that the discouragement of my attending Reed College[37] symbolizes this. My own sense of things was that, after all, I wasn't going to screw up my life by going there, so why not take advantage of an opportunity that was being presented to me? On the

35. Capps, *The Child's Song*.

36. See, for example, Greven, *Spare the Rod*.

37. Capps informed me that a teacher had indicated to him that she could get him a scholarship at Reed College, but his mother opposed this idea because she believed Reed was "overrun by Communists." Capps also noted that this was during the McCarthy Committee hearings, which were targeting professors at various colleges and universities across the country. Personal Correspondence, November 3, 2013.

> other hand, I didn't want to defy her because I knew that if I did, I would probably go into it half-heartedly and, for all I knew, she *could* be right . . . . It might be boiled down to this: (1) The desire to challenge: "What makes you the authority?" (2) The reasonable doubt: "But maybe she's got a point." (3) The resolution: "Let's see if I can figure out a way to keep her happy so that I can get on with my life." But I don't think there is anything especially unique in this; in fact, by citing Stafford's poems, I imply that it's probably rather common among mothers and sons.[38]

Capps's reason for writing about child abuse, then, was not because he felt that he suffered anything extraordinary.[39]

One story from Capps's childhood (one, I think, that is relevant for his portrait of Jesus) involves his younger brother. He writes:

> I was nine years old. My younger brother, then four, had been unusually difficult that day. When my father came home from work, my mother told him about my little brother, how he was becoming more than she could handle. At dinner that evening we—my brothers and I—could feel the tension. No one was speaking. A sense of doom was in the air. After dinner my parents told all of us to stay close. We were not to go running off. Then my father pulled the car out of the garage and my mother came out of the house. They directed us to get in the car, my younger brother between my parents in the front seat and my two older brothers and I in the back. My father pulled out of the driveway and up the street. "Where are we going?" one of us had the courage to ask. No answer. My father drove on. Dusk was approaching. Then, on our right, we recognized the building and began to realize what was going on. We felt dread in the pits of our stomachs. It was the orphanage, and our parents were about to send my little brother away. My father stopped the car and turned to my brother and said, "This is the end of the line." My mother opened the door and began to get out so that my brother could follow. The three of us in the back were stunned. I somehow found my voice and, amid sobs, pleaded: "Don't send him away. He'll be good. Just give him a second chance."[40]

Capps continues:

38. Personal Correspondence, May 29, 2008.

39. Capps writes about various stories from his childhood not as stories of abuse but rather as "less-dramatic" stories. See Capps, *The Decades*, 17–19.

40. Capps, *The Child's Song*, 169–170.

> What I did not know, of course, is that they had no intention of leaving him at the orphanage that night. Years later he told me that he suspected it was a ruse because he noticed that no lights were burning on the first floor of the orphanage, suggesting to him that the offices were closed for the evening. But *I* took them at their word, first believing that they were going to abandon him; next assuming that my pleading in his behalf had made them change their minds. For a very long time—months, maybe even years—I assumed that my parents were capable of abandoning a child of theirs, and I did all in my power to make certain that it would never be me. But something surely died in me—in all of us—that night. Life before that night had not been perfect. There had been the usual conflicts between parents and children, the usual fightings and reconciliations. But this was different. This was the threat of abandonment. The sense of dread that this threat produced in me was nearly overwhelming.[41]

Capps realizes that his brother had provoked their parents beyond their patience and endurance, and that it is possible that his parents had good reason to believe that if they did not take decisive action then and there they would come to regret it in the future. Yet despite these realities, or perhaps because of them, Capps's reflections here come across as melancholy and tragic. Indeed, his orientation toward his parents (and, presumably, toward God) became deeply influenced by this event, as he developed into a boy who did all in his power to make certain that he would never be abandoned to the orphanage: He would be a good boy.

The Image of God

In *Losers, Loners, and Rebels: The Spiritual Struggles of Boys*, which Capps co-authored with Robert Dykstra and Allan Hugh Cole Jr., Capps writes about his adolescence.[42] This work, as well as the sequel *The Faith and Friendships of Teenage Boys* (which is also co-authored with Dykstra and Cole Jr.), comprises some of his most personal (i.e., autobiographical) work to date.[43]

One story that Capps focuses on involves his maternal grandfather, a Swedish immigrant who fathered three girls and one boy. When Capps's

41. Ibid., 170.

42. Dykstra, Cole Jr., and Capps, *Losers, Loners, and Rebels.*

43. Dykstra, Cole Jr., and Capps, *The Faith and Friendships of Teenage Boys.*

mother was thirteen years old, her father died in an explosion at the plant where he worked in south Omaha. Capps's mother told Capps that a week before he died he had had a religious conversion; she took this as evidence that God was at work. On these events, Capps writes: "Although I never knew my maternal grandfather, this story about his conversion experience and his subsequent death in an explosion had a sobering effect on me as a boy."[44]

In graduate school, Capps came to realize how stories such as the one about his maternal grandfather affected his religious sensibility. When reading the writings of psychologist Henry A. Murray, these lines stood out to him:

> Of all these progenitors I was acquainted only with my daughter-venerated grandfather, aloof toward me, but a kindly gent whose white bearded visage resembled God's as painted, say, by Tintoretto. Remembering him I have been led to surmise that the image and concept of Yahweh must have come not from the all-too-familiar father figure, but from the more remote and lordly grandfather, the overruling patriarch of the clan.[45]

Capps added: "I realized that my own understanding of the divine Father was based on stories my mother had told me about my grandfather, a man whom I knew by hearsay only."[46]

Capps also notes that he read Erik Erikson's "Reflections on the American Identity,"[47] and that this essay, too, proved to be important for him. In this essay, Erikson puts forth his view that the boy's male ideal (which is given to him by his mother) is usually not his father but often a grandfather or uncle. Reflecting on Erikson's observations, Capps notes that his maternal grandfather seemed more courageous than his father because his maternal grandfather immigrated and Capps's father, in contrast, did not even fight in World War II (as Capps's uncles had). On his image of God, Capps further observes:

44. Dykstra, Cole Jr., and Capps, *Losers, Loners, and Rebels*, 141. Capps also informed me that his paternal grandfather lived with the family during his boyhood and adolescence, and that, while there were things that he admired about this grandfather (especially his relaxed view of religious doctrines), he did not have the mythic qualities of his maternal grandfather simply because he was physically present. Personal Correspondence, November 3, 2013.

45. Dykstra, Cole Jr., and Capps, *Losers, Loners, and Rebels*, 141.

46. Ibid.

47. See Erikson, *Childhood and Society*, 285–325.

> It was not that I consciously identified God as my maternal grandfather, as though I could look at a photograph of him and say, "There's God." There was, however, an experiential link between my maternal grandfather and God, and this link was a sense of the heroic and the dramatic, of something in the works that was much more momentous than the routine life I led day by day in our house on Spencer Street.[48]

Capps continues:

> I wanted to be like Jesus, the loyal son of this powerful Father and to whatever he wanted of me. This was to join, in a sense, the "Salvation Army," to enlist in the "band" of those who had given everything that they were—and possessed—for the sake of the heavenly kingdom and were now looking down upon boys like me from their places in glory, praying that we would make a similar solemn pledge—that we too would enlist, for the battle could not be won unless we too stepped forward.[49]

"The drama and the excitement were in my religious life," Capps writes, "which was also the life of my imagination."[50]

The Desire to Be another Man's Son

In "The Desire to Be another Man's Son," a section in the chapter titled "The Child Jesus as Endangered Self" in *The Child's Song*, Capps employs the introspective method to see if he could feel what it would be like to be an illegitimate child like Jesus. He writes: "This has proved to be a difficult, even painful exercise, as it has necessarily involved recalling experiences in my own childhood which most nearly approximate his experience, realizing, of course, that Jesus'[s] sense of being a child with a deep sense of personal tragedy was always with him, whereas," Capps continues, "my personal grievances against my own life fate were more episodic and less integral to my ontological sense of myself, my core identity."[51] What did Capps discover from this introspection? He describes it this way: "what I discovered in myself was something of the desire . . . to have experienced my own father more forcefully than I did, and to have had a greater sense of

48. Dykstra, Cole Jr., and Capps, *Losers, Loners, and Rebels*, 142.

49. Ibid.

50. Ibid., 143.

51. *The Child's Song*, 112.

his palpable presence and support, counteracting my mother's commanding, if not controlling presence."[52] He also discovered a sense of gratitude toward his father as well, for his dependability and for the personal sacrifices he made for him: "He was, indeed, a kind of Joseph to me, hovering in the background, rather self-preoccupied and not very talkative, but stable and steady, and, above all, a man who was moral without making a special point of it."[53]

As Capps proceeded with his introspection, he came to the dark realization "that it may have been better for this child to have had a different man for his father."[54] This painful insight led him to feel shame not for himself but for one whom he deeply loved: "I also found myself reliving the blame I had placed on my mother for her role in activating this desire to be another man's son, as she frequently belittled her husband in the presence of her children and revealed through her behavior toward the men her sisters had married that she deserved better."[55] He concludes: "I believe this desire to be another man's son was the beginning of my own religious consciousness, as this longing was not directed towards one of my uncles . . . but to the one whom Jesus called Father."[56]

The School Safety Patrol

In sixth grade, Capps was involved in the school safety patrol and was assigned the most strategic position of monitoring: the place adjacent to the school at the intersection with the most traffic. He was also one of the two students who, at the beginning and the end of the day, were responsible for raising and lowering the United States flag—a task that held great honor among the sixth graders. So he took the job very seriously and took great pride in this position because he was elected by his classmates to become lieutenant of the safety patrol (the highest-ranking position) for the seventh grade. However, during the summer, another boy's mother went to the school principal and said that she wanted her son to be the lieutenant, and the principal granted this request. Capps notes that both the principal and the boy's mother may not have realized that this was an elected position,

52. Ibid.
53. Ibid., 112–113.
54. Ibid., 113.
55. Ibid.
56. Ibid.

but, in any case, Capps lost his promotion and was even moved to a post a few blocks away from the school. He eventually quit the patrol because he couldn't endure the fact that another boy came around to check to see if he was at his post. Reflecting on this experience, Capps writes, "the experience created a deep suspicion of how human organizations work."[57]

The Dead Robin

Another event that had a significant impact on the development of Capps's religious life occurred when he was mowing the lawn and found a dead robin. He called for his father, expecting that he would take care of it, which he did. But his father also remarked: "His eye is on the sparrow, but I see a dead robin"[58] (cf. Luke 12:6). Capps writes: "The comment implied, of course, that while God was watching over the sparrow, he had neglected the robin. His tone, though, was matter-of-fact, and not one of mockery or sarcasm. Still, although I wanted to laugh, I checked myself because I thought he was being a little too irreverent."[59] In time Capps, as I will demonstrate below, would incorporate this irony into his own religious and intellectual life.

Racial Attitudes

In "Prejudice, Prodigality, and the Precariousness of Life,"[60] Capps mentions that, when he was a boy, his parents took him and his brothers to hear the Blackstone Brothers, a gospel quartet, at an African-American church near their home. In personal correspondence, Capps mentioned to me that he recalls his father telling him that, when he was a boy, his best friends were two black boys in the neighborhood where he grew up but that he was not allowed to play with them when he and they got older. Capps thinks his father made up for this loss by getting his haircuts at a barbershop frequented by African American men. He enjoyed participating in their jokes and banter, and so he was able to recover some of his childhood in this barbershop. Capps also recalls that his mother devoted an enormous

57. Dykstra, Cole Jr., and Capps, *Losers, Loners, and Rebels*, 167. Also see Capps, "Forty Years with Moses."

58. Dykstra, Cole Jr., and Capps, *Losers, Loners, and Rebels*, 145.

59. Ibid.

60. Capps, "Prejudice, Prodigality, and the Precariousness of Life."

amount of time and energy in soliciting donations from church members to support the church's sponsorship of a medical missionary to Tanzanika (now Tanzania). Capps noted that, while his father's relations with African Americans were more personal than they were for his mother, both helped to instill in him a desire to overcome the dividing line—30th Street—that separated whites and blacks in the city where he grew up. On returning to the city years later, Capps discovered that Malcolm X, whom he admired during the Civil Rights era of the 1960s, had been born a block or so from the dividing line.[61]

PART THREE: APPLYING THE MOURNING RELIGION THESIS

I now want to turn to the relationship between Capps's life and work in light of the mourning religion thesis. To limit my scope, I explore two losses in his childhood, both of which had a religious bearing, that Capps later mourned in his adult life by means of his scholarship. I then move on to demonstrate how his psychobiographical portrait of Jesus helped him to address these losses, and I argue that a key feature of his mourning style became humor.

Two Types of Losses (Stage One of Homans's Theory)

Religious Loss

When Capps was eleven or twelve, he had an experience in a Sunday School class that could have led to disillusionment with regard to religion. His teacher, who happened to be a friend of his parents, predicted that the end of the world was going to happen that year: "He would tell us what a glorious event it would be when Jesus came in clouds of glory and, after a brief battle with Satan and his armed forces, the present world would end and a new world would replace it."[62] Capps was both anxious and excited about the impending apocalypse. He notes that he doesn't remember talking with anyone about this, but adds: "If I talked with anyone about it, this would almost certainly have been my mother, and I doubt that she would have

61. Personal Correspondence, November 3, 2013.

62. Dykstra, Cole Jr., and Capps, *Losers, Loners, and Rebels*, 143.

cast doubt on the teacher's prophesy."[63] The day that the teacher predicted came and went and, of course, nothing happened. The following Sunday the teacher apologized for the miscalculation, and, as Capps recalls, no one made a big deal out of the mistake. While he could have become disillusioned with religion (as a consequence of this failed prophecy), he did not. Indeed, he became even more determined to live a life pleasing to God. However, "If the experience did not lead to disillusionment," Capps writes, "it created wariness with regard to the religious imaginations of others."[64]

To be sure, I am not suggesting that this particular loss was so significant and so devastating that it required decades of mourning; I am offering this, rather, as a kind of personal Weberian "ideal type"[65] of experience that Capps had throughout his life where the religious claims of others were found to be unreliable.

Maternal Loss

Another significant loss involved Capps's relationship with his mother. In articulating his male melancholia theory, Capps argues that men—*all* men—become religious on account of their separation from their mothers, usually between the ages of three and five. By making a claim about *all* men, Capps is, therefore, also making a self-disclosure about himself. As Capps writes in *Men, Religion, and Melancholia*: "I have profited from many personal conversations in recent years with students and colleagues on the topic of this book, but those that especially stand out in my mind are ones I had with John Capps [Capps's son], who sensed by the rather serious tone of our conversations that the topic of melancholy has for me a personal subtext, which mercifully remained, for the most part, unspoken but understood."[66]

While Capps did not provide much autobiographical material when he wrote about male melancholia in *Men, Religion, and Melancholia*, he has, as noted, recently written about his own life in light of this theory. He notes that one way that he dealt with the loss of his mother was reading:

63. Ibid.

64. Ibid., 145.

65. On Max Weber's notion of "ideal types," see Ritzer, *Sociological Theory*, 128–130. Also see Weber, *The Protestant Ethic*.

66. Capps, *Men, Religion, and Melancholia*, xii-xiii.

> As an early adolescent boy, books were for me a compensation for my earlier loss of my sense of my mother's unconditional love, but the Bible was special in this regard, for the Bible was to a Protestant boy what the Mother Church was to a Catholic boy. The Bible was a book that I could hold in my hands, turn its pages, and engage its words with all of my senses and not be concerned that I might cause "her" to be angry, upset, or hurt.[67]

This self-disclosure fits hand-in-glove with the mourning religion thesis: Capps experienced a loss (mother); he found a new object to replace her (the Bible); and he developed a method that would help him to continue to cope and even thrive in the face of the loss (reading). As the boy Capps grew into the man Capps, his methods of coping with loss became more sophisticated, as he went from reading to writing to the creation of theory.

I am not, to be sure, basing a whole stage of Homans's theory on two instances of loss in Capps's life. Rather, in this section I have offered two instances of loss as personal ideal types of losses that Capps faced—namely, religious de-idealization and maternal loss—because these were central to his mourning and subsequent creation of meaning. Toward the end of this chapter, I will explore of a number of other significant losses in Capps's life, thus providing more evidence for stage one of Homans's theory.

Individuation (Stage Two of Homans's Theory)

I now want to turn to stage two of Homans's theory: individuation. My argument is that Capps was able to individuate from the religious de-idealizations that he experienced as he matured as well as his loss of his mother by writing about Jesus in that, in his book on Jesus, he was able to integrate and to sustain two aspects of his identity: his psychology of religion self (which was subversive toward religion) and his pastoral care self (which was supportive of religion). Capps describes these selves in "The Letting Loose of Hope" and notes that his psychology of religion side is "ambitious," "iconoclastic," "anti-traditional," and "the source of novel ideas," whereas his pastoral care self "reflects the self committed to values and ideals" and is "more responsible and mature," "devoted to being genuinely helpful," "more prudent and cautious," and "values tradition."[68]

67. Dykstra, Cole Jr., and Capps, *Losers, Loners, and Rebels*, 154–155.

68. Capps, "The Letting Loose of Hope," 139.

Capps's Psychology of Religion Self in Jesus

As discussed above, a major component of Capps's portrait of Jesus deals with how Jesus healed. To some readers, this is perhaps the most controversial aspect of Capps's portrait, as he offers psychological explanations for what many religious believers consider to be miracles. Drawing on Freud's writings, Capps argues that Jesus was able to heal by means of his words: "I conclude that there was, indeed, an element of magic in Jesus'[s] exorcisms, based on the fact that, for children, words *were* originally magic, especially those that involved reversal of sound."[69] In other words, Jesus healed in the same way that a gifted psychotherapist heals (i.e., words) and not by means of supernatural miracles. Jesus was, then, a kind of ancient village psychiatrist.[70]

By offering this realistic (and perhaps even reductionist) interpretation of the healings of Jesus, I suggest Capps was able to honor his psychology of religion self when the stakes were the highest for him as a Christian author. If as a psychologist of religion Capps would make explanatory interpretations of other religions (or of minor figures in his own religious tradition) it would seem that his work would lack a certain courage or authenticity. But Capps *did* have the courage to be consistent in his methodology, and he was thus faithful to himself in his search for a more reliable truth.

Capps's Pastoral Care Self in Jesus

Capps's portrait also has a pastoral emphasis. He writes: "Our portrait of Jesus thus concludes on the theme of faith, hardly a novel conclusion."[71] He views faith here as the opposite of anxiety, and cites as an example Jesus's inner calm when he was on a boat during a storm (cf. Mark 4:37–40). He believes that this story would have been the perfect image to have of Jesus after the temple disturbance, for it would capture "the 'inner calm' of the man who had at last triumphed over reproachings without and within through this culminating act of healing. It is the inner act of self-exorcism. Dare one imagine that as he stood in the temple court, awaiting arrest, he raised his face to the heavens and said, 'It is finished'?"[72]

69. Capps, *Jesus*, 192.

70. See Capps, *Jesus the Village Psychiatrist.*

71. Capps, *Jesus*, 262.

72. Ibid., 263.

This suggestion—the suggestion that Jesus said "It is finished" with respect to the temple disturbance rather than on the cross (cf. John 19:30)—is a critique of the Jesus of atonement theology, which maintains that the death of Jesus on the cross is salvific.[73] Capps, instead of focusing on Jesus's death, focuses on what Jesus *did* (i.e. cause a disturbance in the temple), not *what was done to him* (i.e., Jesus's crucifixion), as he believes that Jesus's actions in the temple—and not his death on the cross—can be salvific for us.

Integrating and Sustaining the Psychological and the Pastoral

In the dedication of *Jesus*, Capps writes: "In the course of writing this book, I was mindful of the desire to keep faith with [my boyhood self] and have done so, I believe, by striving to write a study of Jesus that was not afraid to ask questions in search of *a more reliable truth*. This book is dedicated to him."[74] The fact that he dedicated the book to himself intimates the personal nature of the book, and the fact that he feels that he needs to search for a more reliable truth suggests that he found some religious claims, such as his teacher's false prophesy (though surely more than just this one), to be *unreliable*. This dedication suggests that he is setting out to set the record straight with regard to his childhood and his religious life. In this sense, the writing of *Jesus* can be seen as an act of individuation.

I noted above that Capps's male melancholia theory is deeply personal for him. His book on Jesus is also deeply personal in that he applies this theory to Jesus, and the result of such self-reflexive writing is that Capps's portrait of Jesus is highly creative. Indeed, one can observe specific passages in the book that are interpretations only he could make. For example, in offering a psychological explanation for the healing of a possessed boy (Mark 9:14–29), a passage discussed above, Capps, as noted, speculates that the demon-possessed boy was attacking his internalized mother by means of fits that resembled epilepsy. A few paragraphs after Capps explores the maternal subtext of this boy's experience, he makes an observation that has an unquestionable affinity with his own childhood when he notes Jesus's indignant response to the boy's father because he doubted Jesus's ability to heal his son. Capps writes: "Jesus'[s] 'indignant' response to the father, especially in light of his own experience of fathers, seems to imply, 'Why do you expect me to succeed where you have failed?' Thus, it may well have

73. See Rita Brock and Rebecca Parker, *Proverbs of Ashes*.

74. Capps, *Jesus*, xiii, emphasis mine.

communicated a veiled critique of fathers who seem powerless to provide their sons genuine assistance into manhood."[75] This insight into the text—the insight that Jesus, a fatherless son, is critiquing a father for not helping his son to navigate his way into manhood—comes from a man who wished to have experienced his own father more forcefully and from a man who experienced his mother as dissatisfied with her life and felt powerless to make her happy.[76] While Jesus succeeded in saving his mother (by cleansing the temple), Capps could not, unless Capps's portrait of Jesus saving his mother is read as an expression of Capps saving his own mother. In any case, I suggest that Capps's speculations are not arbitrary or the product of a detached academic interest in psychoanalysis, and that his portrait of Jesus is highly creative and remarkably original *because* it is personal. I further suggest that Capps's portrait was psychologically helpful for Capps because it helped him to individuate from losses related to his religious life—what, in Capps's words, we might call unreliable truth—by providing him a means to sustain and to integrate his psychology of religion self and his pastoral care self. If his psychology of religion self deconstructs unreliable truth, his pastoral care self reconstructs a more reliable truth—and all of this deconstructing and reconstructing is done in deeply personal ways for Capps.

A Creative Turn to Humor (Stage Three of Homans's Theory)

Stage three of Homans's theory involves the creation of new meaning. I suggest that Capps's creation of his male melancholia theory was a creative response to various frustrations and losses with regard to religion and to his mother; that his creative response took place over a number of years (the late 1990s and the early 2000s); and that the marker of his turning melancholia into mourning is indicated by his writings on humor.

It is important to note that Capps developed the male melancholia theory over time. In *Men, Religion, and Melancholia*, published in 1997,

75. Ibid., 176.

76. Capps informed me that, when his mother suffered a massive stroke in her late sixties, the worries and anxieties that she had manifested throughout her life disappeared. In her letters, she wrote about the sun, the birds, and other natural phenomena. Capps also noted that during this period she did not seem to think about God. Capps concluded that what he had been unable to do—i.e., to find a way to make her happy—the stroke had achieved, and that this experience, for Capps, helped to reinforce his sense of the ironies of life. Personal Correspondence, November 3, 2013.

he did not frame his analysis in terms of typologies (i.e., honor, hope, and humor); indeed, he wrote only in terms of maternal loss, though the themes of honor and hope were implicit in his analysis. After writing *Jesus* (published in 2000), he posited the typologies of honor, hope, and humor in *Men and Their Religion*, published in 2002, but even then the theme of humor was only addressed in a short concluding chapter. So I suggest in terms of Homans's theory that Capps's creative response did not occur all at once but rather over a number of years; Capps was able to write about humor (his solution to male melancholia) only after he dealt with loss in his religious life, and the key moment in this regard—the moment of individuation—occurred during his writing of *Jesus*.

As time went on, the subject of humor took on a larger role in Capps's writings. To date he has written two monographs on humor and a co-authored book on humor (with his son), as well as a number of articles.[77] In *A Time to Laugh: The Religion of Humor*, Capps notes that "[t]he idea that 'laughter is the best medicine' became a conviction of mine from an early age, but I didn't give this particular belief much thought as I entered adulthood,"[78] and that he did not attempt to "make a systematic argument on behalf of [humor's] capacity to enrich religion, for I believe that an effort to do so would lead to the sorts of generalizations and abstractions that theologians tend to delight in but that leave more ordinary religious people gasping for air."[79]

It is striking that Capps speaks of the *religion* of humor. To me this suggests that Capps never leaves religion behind in his search for a more reliable truth; he uses humor to restore it or, to use his own language, to reframe it. By studying religion professionally, he *did* find a more reliable truth by constructing his own portrait of Jesus. After constructing this portrait, I suggest that Capps's turn to humor was instrumental in and reflective of a transformation in this mourning process because humor allowed him to integrate his professional identities further in that humor has a subversive and iconoclastic aspect (which fit with his psychology of religion self) and a nurturing aspect (which fit with his pastoral care self).

77. See Capps, *A Time to Laugh*; Capps, *Laughter Ever After*; Capps and Capps, *You've Got to Be Kidding*; Capps, "The Psychological Benefits of Humor."

78. Capps, *A Time to Laugh*, 1.

79. Ibid., 169.

The Timing of Capps's Transformation: Writing through Loss

When did this transformation—i.e., the transformation of turning melancholia into mourning—occur in Capps? I suggest that it occurred during his sixties. This suggestion is supported by looking at the dates of some of his most personal publications. Capps was fifty-six years old in 1995, the year he published *The Child's Song* (which, even to this day, is arguably his most sustained critique of religion). He next put forth his male melancholia theory in 1997. He published his psychobiography of Jesus in 2000. He added the typology of humor to his male melancholia theory in 2002. And in 2005 he published his first book on humor, following with another in 2008 and a co-authored book on humor with his son in 2009. There is nothing humorous about religion in *The Child's Song*, and there is little seriousness in *Laughter Ever After* with regard to religion—something changed in Capps between the years 1995 and 2008.

PART FOUR: REACTION AND REFLECTION

I suggest that Capps's fifties were a time in which he was doing serious personal psychological work, as this was the time when he was creating his male melancholia theory. But why did Capps confront these issues when he did? In 1990, when Capps was 51, his father died. This loss, too, would have recalled the death of one of his mentors, Paul Pruyser, who died in 1987. It is striking that Capps, immediately after the death of his father, began a process that resulted in his most creative and original intellectual achievement (his male melancholia theory) just as Freud, after the death of his own father, began a process that resulted in his own most significant achievement (psychoanalysis). When I asked Capps about this, he replied:

> I'm trying to figure out why I got interested in melancholy in my fifties. I know it's too easy to say simply that the books I was using in my course in psychology of religion (the ones featured in *Men, Religion, and Melancholia*) pointed me to the idea, as there must have had to be some subjective receptivity to the idea. It may be, as you suggest, that my father's death was a major personal factor . . . . But, if so, this was also the time when I was teaching a course on pastoral care of men, and I was hearing and reading many stories by the men in the class about how their relations with their fathers were never quite what they promised. I suppose I would place myself in the same category except that I felt that early in life (who

knows when) I accepted the fact that I was not his "favorite" son. I don't think I had any resentment about this. It simply seemed that this was right and as it should be because I was not one of the oldest. But I had several good memories of him and adopted many of his values—to a greater extent, I think, than my other brothers did. Another factor, one that I do, in fact, allude to in the preface, is my relationship to my son. The 1990s would have been the time when he was no longer around—he began college in 1987 and was in graduate school when I was working on the melancholia theme. I know that I missed having him around.[80]

Capps continues,

> Still, reading Freud's "Mourning and Melancholia" at much the same time that I was writing *The Child's Song* and feeling certain that Freud was really referring to mothers (not fathers) was simply an important insight for me. No doubt, I was reacting against the "don't blame mothers" emphasis in the pastoral theology literature at the time, so there was obviously a bit of perversity in my decision to focus on mothers. Also, this was the time when so many of the books on men were emphasizing the father-son relationship, so I probably wanted to distance myself from that literature as well, especially because so many of the men who were writing these books had nothing very critical to say about their own mothers (if I had known of Freud's distinction between denial and disavowal at the time, I would certainly have used it in this case). At this time, too, I was teaching a course on poetry and the care of souls . . . and I was pretty impressed with William Stafford's comment in a video I showed in class about how he had "slandered" his father and mother in his poetry, noting that the poems simply seemed to require it. I found this both rather amusing and liberating—why not "blame" mothers, my own included? Aren't they and our positive memories of them strong enough to take it?[81]

Capps concludes:

> What I think I'm suggesting here is that my father's death and the absence of my son from day-to-day relating were certainly factors

80. Personal Correspondence, September 6, 2008.

81. Personal Correspondence, September 6, 2008. Regarding *The Poet's Gift*, Capps turned to poetry after he had suffered a detached retina. Since the print of poems is usually larger and because there is often a space between each line, he could read poetry better than he could academic books. *The Poet's Gift*, then, was also the product of loss, the temporary partial loss of his eyesight.

> in my writing on melancholia, and I tried to say something about this in the last chapter of *Men, Religion, and Melancholia*. Yet I think I read Harold Bloom's *The Anxiety of Influence* around that time and I was really impressed with his argument that poets (he was talking I think about the Romantics in particular) wrote in response to earlier poets, not primarily out of their own experience—in other words, previous works of literature (trying to compete with Keats, for example) were more important in their work than, say, their own ramblings out into the countryside. It struck me that so much of my own life has been book-related and that I write books based on other books. This may weaken your efforts to relate my writings on melancholia to personal experiences but reading books are—or can be—as powerful of personal experiences as familial events, significant as these clearly are. Why book reading became so important to me as a boy is an intriguing psychological question for me. I don't think it was merely escapist. I now like to say that we would all be in dire straights if we had to rely on what our own society today offers us culturally speaking, and maybe I had some sort of intuition about this when I was younger. So maybe there's a connection to be made between being a reader of books and being melancholic.[82]

There is a lot of material to think about here. I include these long quotations because I think it is helpful for the reader and fair to Capps to include his reactions to my interpretation of his life and work. While I do not want to sort through the various points that he makes here, I do want to emphasize his comment that much of his life has been book-related and that he writes books based on other books: One simply cannot overestimate the importance of reading for Capps; reading holds a place of religious significance in his life.

Capps experienced other losses near or during his fifties that would have prompted him to take on the melancholia issue. Erik Erikson, whom Capps greatly admired and with whom he even had the chance to talk in Erikson's house, died in 1994; Capps's brother, Walter Capps, died in 1997; and his mother died in 1981, the year that he was on sabbatical from Phillips Theological Seminary at Princeton Theological Seminary. Capps writes:

> I recall feeling some regret that she did not know that I would probably be offered a position at [Princeton Theological Seminary] as I didn't want my parents to know about it until it was definite. I also recall that I was teaching Levinson at the time and

82. Personal Correspondence, September 6, 2008.

> that I was therefore in the mid-life transition (forty-two years old). He says that persons at that age often experience the mortality issue through deaths of family members or friends. I think that my interest in narcissism was strong at the time so that I didn't get around to melancholia until later, but it's probably the case that it dates back to her death.[83]

CONCLUSION: REFRAMING RELIGION

In this book I am interested in what I am broadly calling reversals and restorations of religion, as I argue that each of my subjects reverse and restore religion in their own way and in their own language. The language that seems most appropriate for Capps seems to be the reframing of religion. This is because the language of reframing captures the ways in which Capps attempted to restore religion, and because it is a language faithful to Capps's own writings.[84] While, for example, Capps found the Jesus of traditional Christianity to be unreliable (e.g., the Jesus of atonement theology), which can be viewed as stage one of Homans's theory, he was able to take the same basic data about Jesus and to see it through a new frame—the frame of psychological analysis—and by so doing was able to find a more reliable truth, which can be viewed as stage two of Homans's theory. This truth was more reliable for Capps because it integrated and sustained in a personal way his psychological and pastoral selves. Evidence in this regard includes statements such as these that integrate Freud (reflective of his psychology of religion self) and Jesus (reflective of his pastoral care self): "Paraphrasing Freud's oft-stated observation that dreams are the royal road to the unconscious, humor is the royal road to the [K]ingdom of God."[85] As demonstrated by this quotation, Capps is still clearly religious as a psychologist of religion, but his religiosity is one that welcomes Freud and psychoanalysis.

I have argued that Capps was prompted to address his melancholia in his fifties because it was at this general period of his life that he experienced a number of losses, such as his son leaving for college, the death of his father, the death of his brother, the death of Paul Pruyser, and the death of Erik Erikson. These personal experiences also affected his choice of reading, and the most important with regard to my thesis was his reading of

83. Personal Correspondence, September 12, 2008.

84. See Capps, *Reframing*.

85. Capps, *A Time to Laugh*, 170.

Freud's "Mourning and Melancholia"—an interest that dates to the death of his mother—because it led to the development of his male melancholia theory (stage three of Homans's theory), a theory that was later applied to Jesus and subsequently developed and refined for nearly two decades afterward.

It seems fitting to end this chapter by quoting the first line of the epigram for *Men, Religion, and Melancholia*: "My mother did not want me to be born."[86] It occurs to me that the poem from which this line is taken would have spoken deeply to a man who knew that he was not his father's favorite son and who felt emotionally abandoned by his mother. Is it any wonder that this boy grew up to create a portrait of Jesus that emphasized Jesus's own ambivalent relationship with Mary and Joseph? This reframed Jesus showed Capps a Father in whom he could find a more reliable truth.[87]

86. Capps, *Men, Religion, and Melancholia*, vii. Capps mentioned to me that this statement, from a poem by Galway Kinnell, seems a bit histrionic to him but that he *did* learn that, after his father's death (nine years after his mother died) that she had wanted her third child to be a girl. Capps added, "Although she never intimated to me that I was not the child she had wanted, I suspect that I had an intuitive sense that she would very much have liked to have a daughter with whom she could share womanly interests. Many men are 'disappointments' to their mothers in this sense, and I would guess that their melancholia may thus be traced to a circumstance over which they have no control or power to overcome or repair." Personal Correspondence, November 3, 2013.

87. As noted in the epigram for this chapter, Capps's favorite Bible verse as a boy and youth was John 14:6: "Jesus said to him, 'I am the way, and the truth, and the life. No one comes to the Father except by me.'" Capps mentioned to me that, while "coming to the Father" was very important to him, it is noteworthy to him now that "the truth" is the middle term between "the way" and "the life," as if to suggest that finding one's way and experiencing life depend on realizing the truth about oneself.

3

Recalling Religion

> There still exists a conspiracy of dishonesty in our religious studies classrooms, the pretense that students, and teachers, and authors are not provoked into the "study" of religion by their own personal religious questioning (or else that the personal questioning can be held irrelevant to the study). With supreme irony, we invoke the authority of the humanities to dehumanize ourselves, our students, our authors, and their authority by consigning personal religious quest to the closet or the corridors or the chapel.[1]
>
> —James Dittes

INTRODUCTION

James E. Dittes (1926–2009), Roger Squires Professor of Pastoral Counseling at Yale University, was born to Mary Freeman Dittes and Mercein Dittes in Cleveland, Ohio, on December 26, 1926. He married Frances Skinner Dittes in 1948. They had four children together: Larry was born in 1953, Nancy in 1954, Carolyn in 1956, and Joanne in 1958. Larry, who was born with Down syndrome, died from heart complications in 1959. Dittes went through two divorces. He divorced his first wife in 1983. He married Margaret House Rush in 1984, and they divorced in 1986. He married Anne

1. Dittes, "Teaching Freud's Teachings," 269.

Hebert Smith in 1987. In 1994 Dittes was diagnosed with Parkinson's disease. Smith and Dittes remained married until his death in 2009.

For undergraduate study, Dittes matriculated at Oberlin College in 1944 but joined the Navy in 1945 and worked as a radio technician in the Pacific Ocean during World War II. He returned to Oberlin in 1946 and graduated in 1949 with a major in English and American literature. He matriculated at Yale Divinity School in 1949 with an interest in psychology. After the first year, however, he took a leave of absence and went to Turkey to teach English. Toward the end of his first year in Turkey, he decided to apply to the doctoral program in the psychology department at Yale University. He was admitted. So when he returned he was both a doctoral student in the psychology department and what we would today call a Master of Divinity student in the Divinity School (it was then called a Bachelor of Divinity degree). He received his BD in 1955. He finished his doctoral degree in 1958 and was appointed to a position at Yale as Assistant Professor of Psychology of Religion. He moved through the ranks and became Professor in 1968. When he procured the rank of Full Professor at the age of forty-two, he was also given appointments in the Department of Psychology and the Department of Religious Studies. Dittes also served as Director of Graduate Studies from 1969 to 1975 (and intermittently from 1985 to 2001), as well as Chair of the Department from 1975 to 1982. He was also an active member of the Society for the Scientific Study of Religion, as he served as Editor of the Society's journal from 1966 to 1971 and as President of the Society from 1972 to 1973.[2]

The focus of this chapter is on Dittes's psychological portraits of St. Augustine of Hippo (354–430) and how his personal experience influenced these portraits of Augustine. Augustine is well known for many reasons, especially for his ideas relating to original sin and just war theory. He is well known, too, for writing the first western religious autobiography, the *Confessions*.[3] Of interest, he also greatly influenced John Calvin, who is a subject of the next chapter. This chapter will have four main parts: part one will present Dittes's psychological portraits of Augustine; part two will present autobiographical and biographical information concerning Dittes's life; part three will explore the themes of grief and mourning in Dittes's

2. The biographical information on Dittes's life presented thus far is taken from Capps, "James E. Dittes." Also see Carlin, "Dittes, James."

3. Augustine, *Confessions*.

publications; and part four will identify and explore continuities between the life and thought of Dittes (i.e., apply the mourning religion thesis).

PART ONE: DITTES'S PSYCHOLOGICAL PORTRAIT OF AUGUSTINE

In the previous chapter, I focused on a psychobiographical monograph. In this chapter I focus on two essays in an edited volume on the psychological study of Augustine's *Confessions*.[4] Since these two essays focus on the *Confessions*, they are methodologically different from the psychobiographical monograph on Jesus because (1) they do not focus on the whole life of Augustine—indeed, the *Confessions* focus on the first thirty-three years of a man who lived to be seventy-six; and (2) they do not draw on historical and biographical data outside of the *Confessions*. So the nature of this psychological portrait of Augustine is very different from the other two psychological portraits explored in this book.

Continuities between the Life and Thought of Augustine

"Continuities between the Life and Thought of Augustine" is Dittes's first essay on Augustine in the volume.[5] It was first published in 1965. He begins the essay by noting that Augustine's intellectual context—the Mediterranean world of the fourth century—was one rich with choice and that Augustine tested out many of these choices before converting to Christianity in his mid-thirties. Why, Dittes wonders, did Augustine pick the specific form of Christianity that he did? Dittes seeks the answer to this question by identifying and exploring continuities between the life and thought of Augustine.

Elements of Augustine's Thought

Dittes proceeds by identifying six key elements of Augustine's thought. The first is that Augustine adopted a neo-Platonic understanding of the structure of the universe and emphasized God's creative and sovereign functions. Being and goodness, Augustine argued, emanate from God

4. Capps and Dittes, *The Hunger of the Heart*.

5. Dittes, "Continuities between the Life and Thought of Augustine."

and all emanations from God, such as the world and human beings, do not have independent existence but rather are dependent on God and are imperfect. The second is that, comparatively speaking, Augustine did not emphasize the figure of Christ as a mediator or as a redemptive agent. The third is that the Church becomes the ultimate authority. The fourth follows from the first and concerns the problem of evil in neo-Platonic thought: Evil is not a dynamic substance but is the absence of good. The fifth involves the question of human freedom, particularly as resulting from his debate with Pelagius (who made a strong case for free will), and Augustine argued against Pelagius that the fate of a human being is completely dependent upon the will of God. In other words, Augustine substantially limits the possibilities of free will. The sixth involved his debates with the Donatists. The Donatists believed that the effectiveness of the sacraments was dependent upon the moral actions and status of the persons administering the sacraments, meaning that the sacraments administered by a corrupt priest, therefore, were not valid. Augustine argued, in face of this view, that the sacraments received their validity from God's being and status, not the actions and status of human beings. All six of these features of Augustine's thought, Dittes suggests, rest on the "utter dependence of man on God, his own virtual impotence and ineffectiveness before God," and that a "parallel theme is that of remoteness, aloofness, absoluteness, impersonality, [i]napproachability—except in abject humility of confession—of this controlling God."[6]

Internal Conflicts

Dittes next turns to a discussion of Augustine's early life. Noting that Augustine was a firstborn son of a young woman and an older father who was aloof, he argues that Augustine and his mother had an especially strong attachment that created an internal conflict in him with regard to his needs for independence and autonomy on the one hand, and dependency and attachment on the other. Dittes offers some rather direct evidence in this regard by pointing out that (1) Monica (his mother) moved into Augustine's household later in life and forced the mother of his child to move out; (2) she sabotaged his marriage plans at least twice; and (3) she shared a mystical experience with him that had erotic overtones. He offers some indirect evidence in this regard as well, such as Augustine's apparent preoccupation

6. Ibid., 122.

with infancy (he devotes three chapters in the *Confessions* to his earliest years) and orality (this theme shows up throughout the *Confessions* in discussions of the breast, a pear, and rhetoric)—themes that have Oedipal and maternal overtones.

Dittes also observes in Augustine a "strong" and "strongly disturbing" conscience, and speculates that this is the result of a strong mother who had become internalized:

> [S]ome troubling, gnawing guilt may be inferred from such elements of the *Confessions* as these: his readiness to blame his errors on others, his peers, his teachers, his parents, and even God; the persevering, compulsive, ritualistic style of the "confessions"—not entirely unlike Martin Luther's well-known, repetitious, unrelenting, but never satisfied confessions in the monastery; his disposition to even invent wrongs to be confessed, the constant ostentatious self-abasement.[7]

Dittes observes that, because Augustine "won" the Oedipal battle on account of his father dying when Augustine was sixteen, his relationship with his mother became all the more anxiety provoking, and Dittes therefore suggests that Augustine developed a deep ambivalence toward his mother that consisted of both love and hostility. But his hostility toward his mother did not—and could not—manifest itself directly but rather was displaced and disguised in various ways. In the *Confessions* this hostility appears in his excessive complaints about his teachers, adults in general, and his father. But Monica's faults, curiously, are not mentioned in his complaints. Indeed, her shortcomings are not noted by Augustine until he prays for the forgiveness of her sins on the occasion of her death; Dittes believes that this conspicuous silence is reflective of Augustine's ambivalence.

Resolution of Conflict

Having explored key elements in Augustine's thought and central conflicts in his life, Dittes now turns to demonstrating how Augustine resolved his personal conflicts by means of his thought as well as his behavior. In Augustine's youth, Dittes observes two ways in which Augustine asserted his independence from his mother. The first way was sexually. Dittes notes that Augustine's adolescent sexuality consisted of about a year of having multiple

7. Ibid., 124.

sexual partners that was followed by about thirteen years of fidelity to his concubine, who was, as noted, eventually evicted by Monica. Augustine then had a relationship with another concubine, until he finally became celibate. Dittes suggests that male sexuality implies "active self-assertive behavior" and points out that his mother disapproved of such sexuality for her son. Dittes observes, on the one hand, that Augustine could have identified with his father in terms of his sexuality but that, on the other hand, he was unable or unwilling to claim the role of a husband—an expression, Dittes argues, of ambivalence. Augustine simply could not or would not adopt what Dittes refers to as an active, self-assertive masculine identity (and identify with his father); nor could he or would he claim celibacy (and identify with his mother).

The second way that Augustine asserted his independence from his mother was intellectually. Dittes discusses in this regard Augustine's engagement with Manichean thought. One important theme in Manichean thought includes the notion that there is a struggle between the forces of good and the forces of evil, and that every individual needs to pick a side because they can literally affect the outcome of the battle. Manichean thought is an active, self-assertive faith. By endorsing this intellectual tradition, Dittes suggests that Augustine was asserting another form of independence, one very different from the faith of his mother. But Augustine eventually came back into the fold, both sexually and intellectually:

> After years of the most vigorous assertion of his independence, Augustine submitted. He surrendered to his mother, and to her church and to her wishes. He abandoned masculine sexuality. He abandoned all active personal striving, including his vocational roles and aspirations. He abandoned those things which his father particularly endorsed and represented. He abandoned, in short, the effort to be a father.[8]

Instead, Dittes suggests, Augustine became "an obedient son."[9] That is, Augustine resolved his conflicts by conforming to the wishes of his mother by submitting to the will of her God.

8. Ibid., 128.

9. This interpretation by Dittes recalls an essay by Freud. See Freud, "A Religious Experience." Also see Carlin, "A Religious Experience."

Augustine's Search for a Fail-Safe God

Dittes's second essay on Augustine, titled "Augustine: The Search for a Fail-Safe God to Trust," was published in 1986. He begins by focusing on Augustine's loss of his best friend and suggests that this depiction of tormented grief is a vivid portrayal of the religious quest: "The soul yearns to pour itself out—but not upon the sand."[10] Dittes elaborates:

> The longing to become totally alive by becoming totally present, unreservedly committed to another, "all there" in firmly reliable bond, to love God with the whole heart, whole soul, whole mind . . . this is the religious impulse.[11]

But the religious dilemma is how to find something worthy of such commitment—how to find something that is fail-safe? This is the central question of Dittes's second essay on Augustine.

Dittes observes that everything for Augustine turned out, in the end, to be untrustworthy—parents, teachers, mentors, students, friends, lovers, and ambitions—and that the theme of disappointment runs through all of his personal relationships and goals. Nothing in this world is fail-safe. And so, Dittes further observes, Augustine turned to the tools of neo-Platonic philosophy to find a fail-safe God in Christianity. His fail-safe God is one who is incorruptible, inviolable, and immutable. Dittes points out that there are other ways to render God fail-safe, such as the way of the pietist (where God is kept close and face to face) as well as the way of the sacramentalist (where God's presence is carefully regulated by pastors and priests and contained in bread and wine), but Augustine's way of rending God fail-safe was by keeping God distant: "The God rendered fail-safe by remoteness permits thereby some intimacy—but an intimacy rendered more intellectual, abstract, aesthetic than earthy and tender. The cost of no longer pouring the soul out onto sand is, apparently, the distilling of the soul into 'harmonies.'"[12] And such a God is precisely what Augustine needed.

10. Dittes, "Augustine," 258.

11. Ibid.

12. Ibid., 263.

PART TWO: PERSONAL PERSPECTIVES ON DITTES'S LIFE AND WORK

I now want to turn to a discussion of Dittes's personal life and public scholarship. I draw on a special edition of *Pastoral Psychology* dedicated to the career of Dittes as well as personal correspondence with members of Dittes's family. This correspondence includes indirect correspondence with Dittes himself.

Capps's Professional Portrait of Dittes

In 2003 Lewis Rambo, Editor of *Pastoral Psychology*, dedicated a double-issue of the journal to the career of Dittes. Donald Capps and Robert Dykstra served as guest editors for the issue. Capps offered "a professional portrait" of Dittes that focused primarily on his writings.[13] He began his article by noting that Dittes, an only child, was born on December 26, 1926; that his father, Mercein, did not graduate from high school and became a skilled carpenter and even built a home for the family; and that Dittes was baptized Presbyterian but grew up in a Baptist church because his mother, Mary, was a soloist in the choir of a Baptist church. Regarding these biographical details, "It has probably occurred to the reader," Capps writes, "that a December 26 birthdate, a mother named Mary, and a father whose profession was carpentry would send a powerful message to a young boy that he was predestined to walk in the footsteps of Jesus."[14] Capps continues, "That the 'voice' he heard in church each Sunday was not the authoritative thunderings of a pastor father but the hauntingly beautiful voice of a much-loved mother may also have led some readers to predict, had they known him then, that he would become what he *did* become, one who made a profession (in all senses of the word) of the ministry of care."[15]

Capps discusses Dittes's early years as a psychologist, his relationship with the influential psychotherapist Carl Rogers, his involvement with the Society for the Scientific Study of Religion, and other notable professional achievements. He points out that while Dittes was writing books on ministry he was also writing articles in psychology of religion. The major themes of Dittes's publications include the vocation of ministry, contemporary

13. Capps, "James E. Dittes."

14. Ibid., 18.

15. Ibid.

western male experience, psychological theorists of religion, empirical research in psychology of religion, psychological testing of ministerial candidates, and empirical laboratory research.[16]

Capps also includes material from personal conversations that he had with Dittes. Here I offer a few highlights. Capps asked Dittes if he identified with any of the major psychologists of religion, and Dittes responded that he most identified with William James, because James doesn't "fret" about being accurate. Capps also asked: If you were stuck on an island and only had one book to read, what would it be? Dittes said that it would be Jung's *Memories, Dreams, Reflections*.[17] And Capps asked Dittes about his legacy and what he would like to be remembered for. Dittes responded that "he has tried to focus throughout his career on human relations, and to take special note of what we, individually and collectively, are *avoiding*, for it is in the identification and explanation of these avoidances that we come to know what it means to have faith and to witness to this faith," and that "he has opposed all forms of reductionism, whenever they appear."[18] Capps adds: "On the other hand, such reductionisms have also drawn his attention to that which stands over and against them, and these opposing moves and forces are what he seeks to endorse and embrace."[19] Capps closes his essay by discussing Dittes's legacy for himself and notes that the greatest lesson that Dittes taught him was how to be "a liberated worker."

Dittes on His Vocation

Dittes's article in the special issue of *Pastoral Psychology* is an entirely personal essay without any citations or references.[20] He begins by noting that he did not know the word "psychology" when he matriculated at Oberlin College as an undergraduate student, and that during his final semester in college he took a psychology course that was taught from a behaviorist perspective. He points out that it was a little later when he heard of Freud. Both behaviorism and psychoanalysis, Dittes notes, came to influence him a great deal.

16. See Capps and Dykstra, "Books and Articles by James E. Dittes."
17. Jung, *Memories, Dreams, Reflections*.
18. Capps, "James E. Dittes," 46.
19. Ibid.
20. Dittes, "Some Accidents, Coincidents, and Intents."

Dittes's eagerness for psychology—whether behavioral or psychoanalytic—was not shared by students or faculty when he began at Yale:

> The psychology in seminaries during the first half of the twentieth century was not, as in the latter half, the psychology of the clinic, i.e., attentive, in the wake of a depression, a world war, and Sigmund Freud, to the deeper, darker parts of personality, past, individual differences, and individual extremes. It was the psychology of the classroom, educational psychology, i.e., optimistic, attentive to the emerging, the newly born, the grand future—what William James might have been heard calling the healthy minded, except that William James was not much heard or heeded either. Even William James was too probing and too dark.[21]

Because his psychological interests were not affirmed, Dittes, as he put it, declared "a moratorium" on them by moving to central Asia Minor to teach English to Turkish boys.[22] As it turned out, however, he came upon a library built by the U. S. State Department that had a great number of psychology books and he "soaked them up," thus confirming to himself that he should become a psychologist.

After his two years in Turkey, he returned to Yale to finish his BD and began working on a PhD in psychology (Dittes never chose *between* studying religion and psychology). When he returned, he found that his psychological interests were now affirmed in the Divinity School, and his religious interests were affirmed in the psychology department as well. The psychology department applauded his efforts to "colonize" the Divinity School, and the faculty of the Divinity School saw him as a "scout" on their behalf. Dittes came to name his vocation as "psychologist/religionist." He also referred to his work as "theological anthropology," "pastoral theology," and "pastoral psychology." He notes that his training in a divinity school and in a psychology department did not prepare him to become a pastoral psychologist because, in all his years of training, he never took a course in pastoral counseling or ministry in any form; his first exposure to such courses was when he began to teach them—nor did he have any training in Clinical Pastoral Education (CPE). And although Dittes gave the keynote address at the founding meeting of the American Association of Pastoral Counselors (which took place in 1966 in Houston, Texas), he

21. Ibid., 6.

22. On moratoriums, see Erikson, *Young Man Luther*, 43–44, 99–104. Also see Capps and Carlin, *Living in Limbo*, 45–63.

was not eligible for membership. Yet Dittes came to discover that pastoral psychology was at the heart of everything that he taught about and wrote.

After decades of teaching and writing in pastoral theology, Dittes came to the conclusion that in such matters of religion and psychology:

> There is no knowledge being accumulated. The occasional attempt to manufacture an accumulation or tradition only proves the point. I came to realize that this is not a collective flaw which we all should repent and correct. This is a merit and strength of those of us who work in some version of psychology and religion. This tentativeness, this everyone-needs-to-start-fresh custom, reflects the way things are.[23]

"It's not just that there isn't accumulation and tradition," he continues, it is that "[t]here can't be."[24] Why? It is because in matters of religion and psychology there cannot be closure and codification, for there is always more than meets the eye. He elaborates:

> It is an important discovery that psychology of religion deals with matters that require—not permit, but require—regular return to the foundations of experience for correction and renewal and perspective. It is in the nature of things that meaningful psychology of religion requires—not permits, but requires—enfolding and unfolding of self throughout as part of the study, so we can't do it for each other. Maybe in some endeavors such as carpentry or the poring over scriptures and Talmud by young rabbis, it is important to know first what tradition has accumulated, then build from there.[25]

"But not psychology of religion," Dittes writes, "which is a personalized process regarding a personalized process. You have to plant and tend new seeds every year."[26]

Perhaps relatedly, Dittes also notes that he never really had vocational mentors in the traditional sense. Instead of mentors, he had "sponsors," that is, people who gave him space, encouragement, and endorsement. Such persons included Gordon Allport, H. Richard Niebuhr, Liston Pope, and Seward Hiltner.

23. Dittes, "Some Accidents, Coincidents, and Intents," 13.
24. Ibid.
25. Ibid., 14.
26. Ibid.

Perhaps it is best to close this discussion of Dittes's personal vocational narrative with his own words, reflecting on the central theme, as he sees it, of his writings. What is the central theme of Dittes's writings? He puts it this way:

> I have studied The-ism, and its elusive opposite. I seem not to have got much beyond my doctoral dissertation of half a century ago, entitled, with a pseudo precision that threatens to mock its own thesis, "Effects of changes in self-esteem upon impulsiveness and deliberation in making judgments." I have come only so far perhaps as to clarify the sequence and emphasize the self-assuring function of certitude; that is, mostly what I have studied has reversed the dissertation title and become "the effects of making judgments on self-esteem."[27]

Correspondence

As noted, part of my research into Dittes's life included correspondence with his family, primarily with his daughter Carolyn. When I first wrote to Carolyn in 2008, she informed me that her father was staying at the Health Center at Whitney Center in Hamden, Connecticut, and that communicating with him had become difficult because the symptoms of his Parkinson's disease were very advanced.[28] She wrote:

> One of the consequences of my dad's advancing Parkinson's disease is that he does not really know what he can and cannot do. *None* of us knows, and it changes from day to day, sometimes better, sometimes worse. It is very unpredictable. Dad seems these days to think he can accomplish more than he really can and he even convinces us around him that he can and will, and then when it doesn't happen it is disappointing and frustrating, for everyone.[29]

She also wrote:

> Up until recently the disease seemed to affect him a lot *physically*, but not mentally; his mind was still sharp. He couldn't always communicate what he was thinking, but he was thinking clearly. During my last visit with him this month, it was clear to me that

27. Ibid., 15.
28. Personal Communication, August 11, 2008.
29. Personal Communication, August 25, 2008.

> this has changed and is changing. His mind is mostly *not* the clever, sharp, clear, insightful, witty mind that I associate with my dad. His powerful one-liners, [the ones] that completely re-frame entire situations, are very few and far between now. He is often confused or seems very out-of-it and far away.[30]

Carolyn and I corresponded for a number of months. One of the questions that I asked her about Dittes concerned his religiousness. She wrote that "I would not describe him as traditional or radical, religiously. I'd say he was the opposite of dogmatic."[31] She also noted that "[c]ertain passages of Scripture held meaning for him. For example, when my sisters and dad were burying his mother's ashes, it was important to [d]ad to recite Psalm 23."[32]

Carolyn also wrote about the religiousness of her paternal grandfather, Mercein Dittes, and described him as a gentle, sweet, and kind man. She recalled a story that Dittes would tell about his own childhood. The story involved a time when Dittes went camping with his mother and father. The mosquitoes were particularly fierce, but his father would not swat them away so that they would be attracted to him and not to his wife and son—a sweet and kind story indeed.[33]

Nancy, another of Dittes's daughters, also corresponded with me. I noted above that Dittes's father built a family house—a project with which Dittes helped his father. Nancy informed me that the "project . . . went on for years, starting as a one-room cottage 'get-away' from downtown Cleveland." She added that they "winterized it and added on [to it] to make it their full-time home, where Mercein kept bees and grew Christmas trees and sunflowers in retirement, until they moved to Florida in 1960 or 1961." "Recently," Nancy wrote, "[d]ad gave me the impression that he resented having to work on the house so much, and that there were things that became very annoying about his father." Nancy also wrote to me about how Mercein died in 1972:

> When [d]ad got the call that Mercein was going downhill fast, [d]ad dropped everything (I assume) and hopped on a series of planes and taxis. Alas, Mercein died a very short time (minutes, or an hour?) *before* [d]ad arrived at his bedside, and [d]ad thought

30. Personal Communication, August 11, 2008.
31. Personal Communication, December 20, 2008.
32. Ibid.
33. Personal Communication, April 24, 2009.

> Mercein had controlled that. Jim *said* that he thought Mercein didn't want his son to see him looking so weak and helpless, but I wondered if [d]ad was really hurt, with other thoughts going through his mind.[34]

I asked Carolyn to say a few words about Dittes's relationship with his mother, who died in 1993. Carolyn wrote:

> He tells the story of his mother "taking to her bed for many weeks" when he was around teenage years. Though [d]ad didn't "diagnose" her with categories such as "clinical depression" because such terms were not used during most of her lifetime, I do think that she suffered from some sort of depression much of the time, although she usually presented a "pleasant" front. She could also be very critical in a very quiet, under-the-breath kind of way, again with a smile on her face. Dad got very angry with her when she made comments about his weight gain in the 1970s and 1980s.[35]

Given the fact that Dittes did not write about his mother in his public writings, one might be led to conclude that it was not as influential as other relationships. I suggest, however, that these comments from Carolyn intimate that it is *more* likely that this relationship *was* deeply important to and problematic for him, and her absence in his writings *reinforces*—rather than challenges—this importance.[36]

Another part of my correspondence with Carolyn involved her passing along information to me from his wife Anne. Below are some of the questions that Anne asked Dittes on my behalf, as well as his responses. I would like to conclude this section of the chapter with Dittes's own words:

> Q. Were your parents traditional in their religiousness?
>
> A. My parents were very traditional Baptists. Both sang in the church choir (mother was a soloist) and my father had his own special seat on the last row, and was on several committees and very active in the church. My mother was more involved in the social organizations of the church. They were Republicans who were appalled by Roosevelt.
>
> Q. Would you call yourself a "traditional radical"?

34. Personal Correspondence, April 28, 2009.
35. Personal Correspondence, April 26, 2009.
36. See Capps, *Men and Their Religion*, xii-xiii.

A. More like an outdated radical. I was a far-out radical in line with new ideas that came out in the 1930s (e.g., about birth control and capital punishment.) And some of these were similar to ideas that came out in the 1970s. I took the lead in radical issues when I was at Oberlin and editor of the college newspaper. I preached my first sermon at Oberlin: "Open Mind."

Q. Were your ideas similar to William James's?

A. No, he was more like a "father" to my ideas. He did espouse openness and I was influenced by him; I couldn't say I was in his "school"—he never had one because his main characteristic was "openness."

Q. What led you to Augustine?

A. Chance. I ran two different study grants and got extra money for them. There were six or seven of us in the group and we decided to write papers on Augustine .... About twenty-five years later, Don Capps gathered some of the same group and suggested we write papers on Augustine .... I was somewhat of an authority on Augustine by that time and taught courses at Yale Divinity School .... [I also taught] for the National Endowment for the Humanities a couple of summers comparing Augustine and Jung. I also taught a somewhat controversial course at the Div[inity] School on the Theology of Jung and Freud. I wrote two long papers on Jung's theology that are in the Yale Divinity School library.[37]

A Student's Perspective

I now want to turn to a different perspective on Dittes—a student perspective. Paul Elledge recounts his experience of taking a seminar with Dittes at Yale Divinity School.[38] The seminar, sponsored by the National Endowment for the Humanities, was on the *theologies* of Freud and Jung. When Elledge saw the advertisement for the seminar, he wrote to Dittes expressing his interest in taking it, realizing that it was unlikely that he would be able to do so because he was at a research university (the seminar was intended for college teachers who lacked research facilities). Dittes encouraged him to apply but primed him for disappointment. As it turned out, Dittes was

37. Personal Communication, December 22, 2008.

38. Elledge, "The Professor and the Saint."

able to persuade the National Endowment for the Humanities that Elledge should be able to take the seminar. Elledge writes:

> To this day, I don't know how he persuaded the NEH to act favorably on my application, or why, except that it represented a challenge to his imagination; it gave him a chance to buck the system, to wage a contest of will against higher authority: to act up. It provided an occasion to be different and to encourage difference: it afforded him a struggle, an opportunity to strive. That he strove with the Endowment on my behalf remains one of the great blessings of my professional life.[39]

On the first day of class, which was on July 17, 1986, Dittes asked the seminar participants to say something about themselves. Elledge was the first person to speak and gave a rehearsed answer about his professional interests. Then Dittes asked him if he would add something *personal.* Elledge didn't know what to say. He remembers that Dittes was the last person to go, and that he "opened up spaciously, even confessionally, with details of challenging and failed associations, broken covenants, crushing betrayals, grievous losses, and yet, with a wink, of his high hopes for a new relationship, as it turned out with the woman to become his next wife, then in its initial stage."[40] And so the intimacy of the course progressed rather quickly. A month into the course, Dittes invited Elledge to stay in his condo while he was away for a weekend so that Elledge might have a pleasant atmosphere in which he could work on his seminar paper. In the condo Elledge notes that there was a poster that had the final lines of Tennyson's poem, "Ulysses," which read: "strong in will/To strive, to seek, to find, and not to yield." Elledge writes, "It strikes me now more forcefully than then that these lines capture something of the combativeness, the searching, the restlessness, the struggle with the attractions of both submissiveness and autonomy that Dittes recognized and thoughtfully responded to in Augustine because [the attractions of both submissiveness and autonomy were] reflected in himself."[41]

Elledge spends the next few pages of his article summarizing Dittes's two articles on Augustine, with a few evaluative comments here and there, and then closes his essay by reflecting on the ending of his seminar with Dittes (the seminar concluded with a farewell party in which Dittes and the

39. Ibid., 174.

40. Ibid.

41. Ibid., 178.

seminar participants exchanged gifts). Elledge's account of this seminar reflects, to some extent, what Dittes was like as a professor. From his account we can see that Dittes was personal in the classroom, even more personal than in his writings. One gets the impression that Dittes was a very gracious and generous teacher.

PART THREE: GRIEF AND MOURNING IN DITTES'S PUBLICATIONS

In exploring the relationship between Dittes's life and work, I now want to turn to three sources published by Dittes that I did not discuss above—Dittes's personal and theological reflections on Joseph; his case of "Howard"; and his final academic publication. These sources demonstrate that grief was a central aspect of Dittes's professional thought throughout the latter part of his teaching career.

The Male Predicament

In the dedication of *The Male Predicament*, Dittes writes, "For Mercein and Larry, my father and my son: We never had a chance to say these things to each other."[42] In the preface, he writes: "This book is dedicated to the two important males in my life, my father and my son, with whom I have had to carry on these conversations in the silence of a still grieving heart."[43] He also dedicates the book to some specific professional colleagues as well as to "the women who have shared with me the throes and joys of a now and then liberation."[44]

The title of chapter 1 is "Joseph: Frozen Power" (cf. Matthew 1:18–25). The central metaphor for the chapter is an experience that he had when he was thirteen years old:

> I learned to play Joseph, quite literally, the year I became a teenager. Miss Gardener and Miss Swearer, who produced the Christmas pageant that year, cast me in the lead role, they said, and taught me how to do it just right. Though their script was only one of many in a boy's life, not even the first, not even the most rigid, it was a clean

42. Dittes, *The Male Predicament*, xv.

43. Ibid., xiii.

44. Ibid.

> and spare script, pure manliness, as taught by women—which is how most of us have learned it.[45]

Dittes notes that they enticed him with promises: a big part, an important role, right next to Mary. And he notes that the biblical Joseph, too, had exchanged promises with Mary—she was to become his wife to bear his children—but his expectations, as were Joseph's, were shattered when they were both given the message: "Don't move." Dittes describes how he was instructed to play the role:

> Eyes down, one hand benignly on Mary's shoulder, the other hand out in open receptive gesture, welcoming all pilgrims, I was to freeze, stock-still, the only person in the pageant unmoving and unmoved, the lead role become part of the scenery . . . . Presiding, in charge but uncharged, steadfastly going through the motions without moving a muscle. I stuck it out manfully as Joseph did, the father who was not the father.[46]

Dittes reflects on what this episode might mean for men and what it *did* mean for him: "Learning to be Joseph for Miss Gardner and Miss Swearer, I was learning to be a man for them, and for all whom they spoke, and shaped. For is this not every man's assignment in our culture, that we run in place?"[47] Dittes believes that our culture misleads men by inviting them to be leaders but, at the same time, asking them to lead by "freezing." He elaborates:

> When men believe the promise of top billing, the invitation to be the center of the action, but don't understand that the script requires them to freeze—when they misperceive the promises as the script—then they spend many heartbreaking and ulcer-plagued years trying to make a difference, trying to have impact and effect, trying to leave the world different from the way they found it. Spent, burned, and burnt out, at last they discover what the Miss Gardners and Miss Swearers knew all along, that the script only requires them to freeze, to simulate action, to be prop and scenery for others to act out their pageantry.[48]

45. Ibid., 3.
46. Ibid., 3–4.
47. Ibid., 4.
48. Ibid.

The promises of life made to men, Dittes is suggesting as he is approaching age sixty, are not fulfilled. A man's destiny—his destiny—is not what he thought it would be: Life promised more than it delivered.

Yet Dittes also points out that men are rewarded for playing the role of Joseph. He recalls, from his own experience, that some of the various scripts that have been given to him over the course of his life have come in the form of compliments: "How tidy you keep your lawn," "Your voice sounds so good from the pulpit," "You have such a nice smile and broad shoulders," "You tell jokes well," and "You are so sensitive."[49] To be a man, it was conveyed to Dittes, is to keep one's lawn clean, have a strong voice, have a nice smile, workout so as to have broad shoulders, be funny, and be sensitive. To be a man is to be like Joseph. And to be like Joseph is:

> (1) to yearn for the richness and color and depth of life which you know is your natural birthright and a God-given promise; (2) to be assigned, instead, a task, a fixed role; (3) to adopt that task as yours, that role as you, and to devise ways of sustaining it, to the point of (a) enlisting others into the script implied by your role and assigning them their corresponding tasks and fixed roles, and (b) bringing vigor and energy and imagination into protecting those roles, theirs and yours, from the erosions and ravages of that rich birthright of life, once—and still?—your treasured promise.[50]

To be a man is to be disappointed and disillusioned with one's dreams, but one's dreams, Dittes also paradoxically suggests, can somehow be satisfied if they can be honestly engaged, disappointment and all.

The Case of "Howard"

Dittes published *The Male Predicament*, which contains his theological reflection on Joseph, in 1985, when he was in his late fifties—a time when he was at or near the height of his professional influence. In *Driven by Hope*, published in 1996 (when he was in his late sixties), he continues writing about the various ways in which life is full of disappointment. While Dittes here again is writing abstractly for all men, Capps points out that the preface intimates that the book is speaking about *a* man: himself. Capps writes: "The fact that he informs the reader in the preface that this book 'aspires to be personal and . . . as conversational as the printed page allows,' and invites

49. Ibid., 22.

50. Ibid., 29.

the reader 'to regard what follows as my way of saying *This is how it is with me,*' indicates that [the theme explored in his book] is—and has been—'the most relentless theme' in his life as well."[51] Capps also notes a personal revelation that Dittes made about the case of "Howard" in the book:

> When I happened to mention my own resonance with "Howard" in our recent conversation, Dittes confessed that "Howard's" experience recounted in chapter 4 was his own. So perhaps one may conclude that the author, whoever he may have most resembled in earlier periods of his life, is most clearly present in *this* book in the form of this particular man, "Howard."[52]

Dittes introduces Howard with this story:

> The checkout clerk at the supermarket is confused. Howard can handle that; he knows how to wait patiently. The register readout says $16.72. He has given her a twenty, plus two dimes and two pennies; she owes him three singles and two quarters. This will give him some quarters for parking—one of the simple survival skills he relishes. He realizes he has outpaced this clerk for the moment, but he can wait for her to catch up. He will explain it to her if he has to. But better to let her punch it out on her keypad: *$20.22 received.* The computer will understand him and explain it to her: *$3.50 change.*[53]

But this is not what happened. The clerk assumed that *Howard* was confused:

> She pushes back the coins with exaggerated patience that is impatience. She is polite about it, too polite, as though she is explaining it to a child—or to an old man. "It's only sixteen seventy-two. See"—she points to the figure 16 on the register readout—"that's *less* than twenty dollars." She spells it all out.[54]

Howard comes to interpret her actions in light of his age because, after all, he is shopping in the middle of the day on a weekday, wearing jeans, hasn't shaved, and seems to be fumbling with money. But he is taking it easy because he had worked through the weekend. Dittes notes that Howard, as a middle-class white man, hasn't really been the object of stereotypes over

51. Capps, "James E. Dittes," 39.
52. Ibid., 40.
53. Dittes, *Driven by Hope*, 49.
54. Ibid.

the course of his life but begins to feel as though he is not being treated as a man because he is aging. When the clerk reaches out and touches his hand in order to give him back his change, he feels emasculated because she does not see him as a sexual threat because she touches him as if he were an elderly relative.

Dittes notes that some might see Howard as a victim of a typical man's addiction to achievement, power, mastery, and control, but this would miss the point, because Dittes thinks that men's attempts at mastery and control are better seen as "religious strategies." He writes: "They are a form of a man's aspirations and expectation for a fuller life. They are one way a man tries to claim promises that elude him."[55] "The religious purist," he continues, "can point out, accurately, that Howard's is a false trust," but "it seems more honest and more helpful to Howard to regard his supply of faith as half full, not half empty, to recognize the religious urgency and hope in his lunges to find himself reliably established, the haunting religious quality of his ache for destiny and his sorrow at finding it passing him by."[56] Dittes, as he was nearing retirement, seems to be expressing here in "Howard" his own feeling that destiny has somehow passed him by.

Dittes returns to the case of Howard in his chapter "Pilgrim." In this chapter, Dittes wants to reclaim the metaphor of pilgrimage as a religious model for men and masculinity. In everyday life, Dittes suggests that many men who are well settled in life—in family and in work—often feel unsettled and discontent. Often men are criticized for this adolescent churning, midlife restlessness, and grief of aging, and they are deemed irresponsible, narcissistic, and noncommittal for valuing personal success more than relationships. Dittes, however, wants to make a re-deeming case for the pilgrim—for unsettledness, for yearning, for despair, for hope. The upshot of re-deeming men as pilgrims as opposed to childish and irresponsible is "not to offer rescue from unsettledness . . . but instead to invite men to claim pilgrimage as the primary arena of life," and it "invites men to believe . . . that sublime discontent is at the same time a sublime hope."[57] In other words, men are correctly viewed as unsettled and as discontent but this discontent is well grounded because life is not as it should be, and the pilgrim knows this.

55. Ibid., 53.

56. Ibid.

57. Ibid., 102.

In terms of the case of Howard, Dittes notes that Howard is disturbed not so much by the label "old" but rather by the fact that he is being viewed as "slow," "incompetent," and "helpless." This is so because Howard has been on a pilgrimage to the shrines of "Quick," "Able," and "Helpful." There is nothing wrong with going to these shrines, Dittes suggests, because these shrines do indeed bestow a blessing, but Howard's mistake was that he set up camp there and tried to settle there, therefore no longer remaining a pilgrim; Howard turned the blessings into scripts. In being tied to these shrines, moreover, Howard has neglected other shrines such as "Delight" and perhaps even "Aging."

The final place where Dittes discusses the case of Howard is in the chapter "The Manhood of Living as a Son." "A full term of sonship," he writes, "is the right of every male, son to a father—genuine sonship, not apprenticeship for fatherhood, not a junior manhood, most urgently not a pretend manhood," and adds that a "man needs this term of wholehearted sonship so he can comfortably move beyond it into an adult manhood that is wholehearted, into unmitigated fatherhood."[58] If a man has not had a wholehearted sonship, then he often develops into a pretend manhood, full of charades and insecurity.

But what is sonship? Sonship is living in potential. It is to live with "a promise and a hope that is also a hunger and a yearning, a kind of chronic shadow of his destiny."[59] And since this chronic shadow of potential is indeed painful, the temptation for boys and men is to move beyond it too quickly in an inauthentic manner. "Such a patriarch (all father, no son)," Dittes writes, "tries too hard, works too hard, frets too much, commands too much, judges himself (and others) too cruelly."[60] Dittes relates this discussion to the case of Howard by noting that the episode with the clerk is insulting only if Howard needs to be regarded as super-competent; the situation with her, rather than being an insulting one, could have been an occasion for the freedoms of boyhood. Yet, if something is wrong (e.g., if a clerk gets the change wrong), men often feel as though it is their job, their duty, to fix it, but Dittes notes that boys carry no such expectation. Dittes sees aging, then, as an opportunity to "mature into boyhood."[61]

58. Ibid., 123.

59. Ibid., 124.

60. Ibid., 126.

61. Ibid., 136–137.

It is worth emphasizing, as Dykstra does in his essay on Dittes's life and work, that in *Driven by Hope* Dittes offers a charitable reading of men's experience, but that Dittes was not always so admirable of men.[62] Indeed, Dykstra notes that some kind of transition occurred in Dittes between the years 1987 and 1996. In 1987, when Dittes published *When Work Goes Sour,* he mildly scolded men for making an idol out of work.[63] In 1996, he republished this book with a different title: *Men at Work.*[64] And in the preface to the second edition, Dittes notes that as he reread the book he now feels that he was too hard on men, that there is something to be admired about men: "If we men do make a religion of our work, let us give full appreciation to our talent and our desire, disclosed therein, for being religious. Work may be an unworthy god, but the religious impulse is not unworthy."[65] By 1996, Dittes, it seems, was beginning to mature into boyhood—more on this transition below.

Dittes's Last Academic Words

In "Teaching Freud's Teachings," his final publication, Dittes reflects on what professors ought to tell their students about Freud. He suggests that, according to Freud, every word that is written or spoken is autobiographical, and adds:

> Our most earnest and rigorous efforts at an "objective" accounting—whether of the animate or the inanimate, ideologies and epics, credos and their predicates, the grand or the trivial—every accounting we make is not nearly so self-contained and autonomous as we pretend, but is contingent; it is, in some significant measure, an accounting of ourselves.[66]

To illustrate this point, Dittes traces a motif in Freud's later thought that he finds expressed in *Civilization and Its Discontents*[67] and *Moses and Monotheism.*[68] He suggests that the theme of *Civilization and Its Discontents* is

62. Dykstra, "Maturing into Boyhood."
63. Dittes, *When Work Goes Sour.*
64. Dittes, *Men at Work.*
65. Ibid., 10.
66. Dittes, "Teaching Freud's Teachings," 260.
67. Freud, *Civilization and Its Discontents.*
68. Freud, *Moses and Monotheism.*

that vulnerability leads to pain, suffering, and death, and vulnerability therefore should be avoided; but that the theme of *Moses and Monotheism* is more or less the reverse, that vulnerability can be a path to life and fulfillment. Dittes's reading of *Civilization and Its Discontents* is straightforward: "Life is bleak, unfriendly, and unrewarding, and don't count on being rescued."[69] And so the book is an argument against religion: It is a call for human beings to grow up. Dittes's reading of *Moses and Monotheism* is less straightforward. This is because it is difficult to know what to make of *Moses and Monotheism*, as this text (as noted previously) is one of Freud's least impressive pieces of writing in terms of style, argumentation, and evidence.[70] In terms of argumentation and evidence, for example, Dittes takes on the question as to why Freud would base his argument on a claim by Ernst Sellin—a biblical scholar contemporary with Freud—that Moses was assassinated by his followers because, when Freud was writing, even Sellin himself rejected his own argument *and Freud knew this*. Why, then, would Freud continue with this line of argumentation that would be sure to embarrass the cause of psychoanalysis? Dittes convincingly argues that the writing of *Moses and Monotheism* can only be understood in light of Freud's own biography—that is, Dittes sought continuities between the life and thought of Freud. Dittes notes that Freud was completing the book near the end of his life while he was living in London, and that he was unsure about his legacy, wondering whether psychoanalysis would survive beyond him. He knew that Charles Darwin had been buried in Westminster Abbey—Darwin's legacy was sealed—but where would Freud be buried? What would his legacy be? Would his teachings be honored? Reflecting on these questions, Freud turned to Moses (which wasn't, as discussed in the introduction of this book, the first time Freud turned to Moses). Freud believed that he was, like Moses, "assassinated" by his followers—Adler and Jung—but in writing *Moses and Monotheism* Freud's teachings (like Moses's teachings) would survive precisely because his followers were unfaithful. Why? Dittes explains:

> In Freud's account, the assassination is essential for Moses'[s] legacy to survive and prevail. As every father comes to prevail in the life of his son just as a consequence of the son's murderous wishes, so the once disloyal people eventually atoned for their guilt

69. Dittes, "Teaching Freud's Teachings," 265.

70. Cf. "Editor's Note," Freud, *Moses and Monotheism*, 4–5. Also see Gay, *Freud*, 645–647.

> by conceding adherence to Moses'[s] teachings. This, the motif in Freud's last years, is the motif of his last book. Once this motif is identified, other puzzling or annoying or distracting sections of the book fall into line.[71]

The upshot is that, even if Sellin was historically incorrect, he was *psychologically* correct, so Freud in *Moses and Monotheism* built on Sellin's work in this sense.

Dittes's thesis in this essay is that there is a shift in Freud's writings from a suspicion of vulnerability and dependence (as articulated in *Civilization and Its Discontents*) to an argument for its efficacy (as articulated in *Moses and Monotheism*). Dittes points out that this shift occurs in Freud's writings after Freud's mother dies, leading Dittes to suggest that "Freud now had much less need to protect himself against the traps of dependence and much less need to insist on his own (masculine) independence."[72] It is striking that this interpretation of Freud by Dittes recalls Dittes's interpretation of Augustine.

PART FOUR: APPLYING THE MOURNING RELIGION THESIS

As Dittes sought continuities between the life and thought of Augustine, I seek continuities between the life and thought of Dittes, especially with regard to Dittes's psychological portraits of Augustine and how these portraits helped him to work through grief in his personal life such as the death of his son and his two divorces. Other significant causes for grief include the death of his father (especially in light of the fact that Dittes seems to have believed that his father controlled the timing of his death) and his strained relationship with his mother (especially in light of the fact that she seemed to have suffered from clinical depression). In what follows I apply the mourning religion thesis to Dittes. This application of the mourning religion thesis differs from my application of the theory in the previous chapter in that here I do not apply the theory in terms of stages; this application is more thematic in nature. I explore dependence and independence, trust and risk, and adaptive melancholia.

71. Dittes, "Teaching Freud's Teachings," 267–268.

72. Ibid., 268.

The Theme of Dependence and Independence

In "Continuities between the Life and Thought of Augustine," Dittes, as noted, makes the case that the key elements of Augustine's thought hinge on the theme of dependence and independence, and Dittes views these elements of Augustine's thought in light of his relationship with his mother. While Augustine flirted with independence—both from his mother and from God—he eventually became "an obedient son" and advocated for dependence on God, thus submitting to the will of his mother. In what follows, I will explore two places where the theme of dependence and independence can be observed in Dittes's writings.

One such place involves his writings on men and work. Above I noted that Dykstra observed a transition in Dittes's take on men and work between the years 1987 and 1996—namely, that while in 1987 Dittes mildly scolded men for making an idol out of work in 1996 he praised men for the same behavior because while work may be a false idol the religious impulse behind men's addiction to work is worthy of praise. What happened between 1987 and 1996? Why did Dittes change his assessment? While he was writing *When Work Goes Sour* (published in 1987) he was going through his second divorce, which could lead one to wonder if one reason for his divorce, from Dittes's own point of view, was due to his own addiction to work. It also seems significant that Dittes's mother died in 1993. If Dittes had a strained relationship with his mother (as my correspondence with his family suggests), then it seems plausible that he would have experienced some kind of personal liberation as the result of her death, a liberation that was later reflected in his more gracious take on men in *Driven by Hope* and *Men at Work* (both published in 1996). Could it be that Dittes's mother felt that Dittes worked too much—did she create, in effect, a double-bind for him that both praised him and blamed him for his success in his work life? This suggestion is supported by the fact that, as noted above, Dittes observed a shift in Freud's writings after Freud's mother had died. Also, Dittes married Anne in 1987, and this marriage proved to last. It strikes me that it seems more than plausible to suggest that the fruits of this marriage helped Dittes to heal from the hurts of his previous two marriages, and that through this marriage he was able to accept men—and himself—because of this relationship. There was no longer any need to blame men, or himself, in his writings; he was freed from the judgment of his mother and the pain of his two failed marriages.

In terms of the mourning religion thesis, I suggest that Dittes was working through his grief relating to women and his grief relating to the losses of his son and his father by writing about men's addiction to work. As we have seen, Dittes articulated the losses relating to men in his public writings (as noted in prefaces and dedications), but his losses relating to women were articulated not as openly—indeed, they were sometimes disguised in the form of cases such as "Howard"—perhaps suggesting that they were all the more painful and more difficult to mourn. In any case, the theme of dependence and independence was a key personal theme for him, a central theme that he identified in Augustine's life. My argument is not that Dittes was able to work through this grief by writing "Continuities between the Life and Thought of Augustine," because this essay was first published in 1965. Rather, my argument is that this essay helped Dittes to identify his own personal issues to work through and that the working through would come later. In this sense, Dittes's work on Augustine proved to be a key turning point for him in the mourning process in a similar way to Capps's work on Jesus.

Another place that one can observe the theme of dependence and independence in Dittes's writings involves Dittes's essay "Teaching Freud's Teachings." It is striking that Dittes observed that the central dynamic in Freud's life, as well as Augustine's life, centered on issues of dependence and independence. Now it may be true that the dynamic of dependence and independence was central for Augustine and for Freud—it is not my intent in this book to assess the validity of any particular psychological or other claim made by Capps, Dittes, or Bouwsma—but the fact that Dittes chose to write about this topic (and that he was able to see these dynamics) when contemplating their lives lends a great deal of weight to the assertion that this was a dynamic in his own life as well.

It is worth pointing out that Dittes suggests that when reading the *Confessions* the "reader, feeling so bidden by Augustine, tries to see himself or herself in the story, and so, of course, tries fitting to Augustine theories and interpretations—whether Oedipal, narcissistic, or more subtle—that are, in some sense, self-portraits."[73] And so I suggest that we should believe Dittes on this point because his portrait of Augustine indeed looks like his own self-portrait. Indeed, Dittes's portrait of Augustine's relationship with his mother appears an awful lot like how Carolyn described Dittes's relationship with his mother: "Mary Dittes lived long enough for [d]ad to

73. Capps and Dittes, "Preface," xx.

go through many phases of his relationship with her. At times they seemed close and at other times [d]ad really 'pushed her away' and tended to 'blame' her for some of his struggles and unhappiness."[74] This could just as well be Dittes's description of Augustine and his mother.

The Theme of Trust and Risk

In "Augustine: The Search for a Fail-Safe God to Trust," Dittes asserts that the soul yearns to pour itself out on sturdy ground, that it longs to become totally alive by becoming totally present and unreservedly committed to another, but the religious dilemma is that it is unclear just what will prove to be fail-safe. As noted, Dittes argues that Augustine's solution to this religious dilemma was to render God trustworthy ("fail-safe") by insisting on God's distance. God is wholly other and therefore trustworthy, immovable and therefore sturdy. In what follows, I will explore two places where the theme of trust and risk can be observed in Dittes's writings.

One such place is by observing, as Capps pointed out, that Dittes himself does not accept Augustine's solution to the religious dilemma. In *Minister on the Spot*, Dittes discusses four ways a person can "go out on a limb" (i.e., take risks) in life. The first way is by taking risks in which we are guaranteed a soft landing. Dittes does not think that there is real potential for growth in such risks because the self is not invested and thus not risked. The second way is by taking risks in which the limbs we go out on are completely sturdy—that is, there is no chance of the limb breaking. So again there is no chance for growth. The third way involves obligation or duty. But Dittes is skeptical that this kind of venturing will lead to growth because, although there is real risk (the limb could break), there is not authentic investment: "One goes out on the limb because the going out is important, not because the limb is important."[75] The fourth way is what Dittes calls "assurance is in the breaking." Here, Dittes writes:

> One moves freely into risks and crises because [one] knows that in—and perhaps only in—crisis and disaster is there prospect of new revelation and new creation and new relation . . . . Adam and Eve did not really become selves and neither do children until they risk . . . the freedom which is theirs. Even when the risk turns out badly, as apparently it often does, there is still more real

74. Personal Communication, April 26, 2009.

75. Dittes, *Minister on the Spot*, 100.

> selfhood—which is a kind of faithfulness to the Creator God—than without the risk.[76]

So if Dittes agrees with Augustine that the religious dilemma involves the problem of trust and risk, Dittes does *not* agree with Augustine that the solution to risk is distance. He thinks, in contrast to Augustine, that the solution to risk is moving freely into risk, pouring one's soul out, even on—perhaps especially on—the sand. In terms of the mourning religion thesis, this theological reflection on trust and risk can be seen as related to Dittes's working through issues of trust and risk as they relate to his marriages and divorces: Assurance is in the breaking (or perhaps breaking-up), he tells others; assurance is in the breaking (or perhaps breaking-up), he also seems to be telling himself at a critical period in his relational life.

Another place that one can observe the theme of trust and risk in Dittes's writings is in the final chapter in *The Male Predicament*. Here Dittes focuses on the fact that Joseph lived as a man in exile in that (1) he was forced to flee from Bethlehem to Egypt; and (2) he was an exile in his own home because he was a man who was a father but not the father. Dittes suggests that there are three responses to the various exiles in which men may find themselves. The first is to escape, deny, defy, and reject the claims of wilderness; the second is to accept and surrender to the wilderness; and the third embraces both simultaneously. He advocates for the third and offers this advice to men:

> Play our role heartily, as though it were the real thing, and disdain it with a hearty horse laugh, knowing it isn't. You may be in the role now, thoroughly playing it out, but you are not the role. You may own it, but it doesn't own you. Accept the script, but know you are more than any script. Live out the looseness and freedom of hearty overcommitment.[77]

This, Dittes suggests, is what Joseph did by accepting Jesus as his own son—he played out his role as father heartily. I suggest that this advice offered here in *The Male Predicament* (published in 1985) is relevant to Dittes's portrait of Augustine offered in "Augustine: The Search for a Fail-Safe God to Trust" (published in 1986) because both, in their own way, are dealing with issues of trust and risk, and Dittes is coming down on the side of risk, no matter

76. Ibid.

77. Dittes, *The Male Predicament*, 203.

what the outcome. If men overcommit themselves to their roles, so be it, because the soul needs to pour itself out, even on the sand if necessary.

Or at least so Dittes advocates here. In *The Male Predicament* Dittes is suggesting that men should be free to live out their overcommitment, but in *When Work Goes Sour* (published in 1987) Dittes, as noted, mildly scolds men for being overcommitted to work, making an idol out of work. This leads me to suggest, contra to what Dittes stated that led him to Augustine (i.e., chance), that there was something attractive about Augustine's solution to the religious dilemma. In other words, at roughly the same time Dittes was advising men to live out their overcommitments heartily in *The Male Predicament* he was also mildly scolding them for doing so—this, to me, suggests some degree of ambivalence in Dittes. And so, in terms of the mourning religion thesis, I further suggest that writing about Augustine helped Dittes to work through some of his ambivalences, especially those related to religion. As I will demonstrate below, this working through represents more of a melancholic holding onto religion rather than a mournful moving on from religion.

Adaptive Melancholia

I now want to offer a composite picture of how I think the mourning religion thesis can shed light on the life and work of Dittes. Dittes's relationship with religion was an ambiguous one. For Dittes, religion provided a deep sense of personal destiny. As he writes in *Driven by Hope*:

> Men live a life that feels chronically destined, ever on the verge—intended for something that is never quite arrived at, an unending not-yet, the perpetual pilgrimage of almost, a prolonged tumescence. Something beckons and promises a man but also eludes and teases—something hinted at in the life he knows but something unmistakably beyond, just beyond naming, ever beyond grasping, intimate and sure and yet elusive—that life which is truly his and yet never his. A man treasures his life as a gift, *mourns it as a gift never unwrapped.*[78]

Dittes suggests that men, whether they profess any particular religion or not, are inherently religious and that a key dynamic of their religiosity is that they live in the chronic shadows of destiny. I suggest that the sense of destiny that Dittes personally experienced was rooted, at least in part, in the

78. Dittes, *Driven by Hope*, 3. Emphasis mine.

fact that he was born on December 26 to a Mary and a son of a carpenter. The fact that he was named James, a brother of Jesus, would also seem to be related to his sense of personal destiny. This suggestion is reinforced by the fact that his most extensive and explicitly autobiographical reflection in any of his writings occurs in relationship to the story of Joseph and the birth of Jesus. Throughout his life, Dittes wrote about how life does not turn out to be the way we imagined it would be, the way we hoped it would be, the way we dreamed it would be. Life is full of disappointment. As a consequence, I suggest that Dittes became, to some extent, disillusioned with religion due to its failure to make good on its promises. Life is a gift that is never unwrapped.

Dittes's story, however, is not one of despair and resignation; it is one of hope. Although Dittes to some extent experienced disillusionment with regard to the promises of life (as mediated through religion), he did not, in the end, reject these promises. He did not mourn religion in the sense of leaving it behind. Rather, religion throughout his life continued to be a source of meaning for him, deepening his capacity to mourn, reflected beautifully in this passage:

> Adam looked around Eden and asked, *Is that all there is?* The sorrow of incompleteness is man's from the outset—part of creation, not a symptom of sin or [F]all—just as the sorrow of a blameless life cut short on a cross reveals redemption, not sin. This sorrow of incompleteness, life chronically destined, is what is offered to man as the avenue to wholeness and holiness.[79]

This question—Is that all there is?—of Adam's just as well could have been Dittes's own question when, at the young age of forty-two, he became Full Professor in 1968. As Dittes later puts it in *The Male Predicament* in 1985:

> To be Joseph is to dream of becoming a professor and to live in that dream intently until appointment and tenure are in hand, only to discover that the professional role is so straitened as to be an exile of drudgery: students and public expect you to pronounce and profess, not just search and query; the university expects you to chair committees; the politics of academia requires you to connive; publishers require you to shape your ideas to market needs. The dream has led you into exile from itself.[80]

79. Ibid., 4.

80. Dittes, *The Male Predicament*, 208.

Is that all there is, Adam asked? Is this all there is, Dittes seems to have asked? Religion for Dittes, melancholic though it was, reflected his *ability*—not his inability—to mourn.

In a sense, to suggest that religion aided Dittes in his mourning process runs counter to Homans's mourning religion thesis. But, as previously noted, there is no single mourning religion thesis. I suggest that Bertram Cohler's notion of "adaptive melancholia" (which is a variation of Homans's mourning religion thesis) is helpful in understanding Dittes's relationship with religion and loss.[81] In "Nostalgia and the Disenchantment with Modernity," a chapter in Parsons, Jonte-Pace, and Henking's *Mourning Religion*, Cohler challenges the view that nostalgia is a pathological expression of an inability to mourn and notes that many psychoanalysts often hold a negative attitude toward religion and nostalgia because both, they assume, are escapist. But Cohler believes that nostalgia can be adaptive: "[N]ostalgia is in fact an adaptive solution to the sense of fragmentation produced by significant loss . . . [because] the ability to construct a past that provides a sense of personal coherence fosters enhanced integration and makes it possible for people to deal more effectively with present problems."[82] As an illustration of how melancholia can be adaptive, Cohler discusses the memory books produced during and after the Holocaust: "Memory books created by survivors," he writes, "re-create continuity with the past, reflect and reestablish a sense of coherence, and function in ways that are psychologically soothing."[83] The point of these memory books is to enhance melancholia, *not* to mourn the losses and work through them, because the danger of mourning the Holocaust is that then it might be forgotten. Nostalgia (or adaptive melancholia) is restorative precisely because it *prevents* mourning and *enhances* melancholia.

I suggest that Cohler's notion of adaptive melancholia applies to the continuities between the life and thought of Dittes, especially with regard to Dittes's psychological portrait of Augustine. Dittes, throughout his career, embraced both religion and psychology; he never chose one at the expense of the other. This meant, in practice, that he taught courses on the *theologies* of Freud and Jung, and that he used various *psychologies*, such as those of Freud and Jung, to understand persons such as Augustine. Dittes never left religion behind in a similar way that many Jews today do not

81. Cohler, "Nostalgia."

82. Ibid., 201.

83. Ibid., 202. Also see Boym, *The Future of Nostalgia*.

leave the Holocaust behind. But neither did Dittes fully embrace religion in some kind of rigid orthodox way. This is apparent in his embrace of Augustine. While large portions of the Christian tradition have to a great extent endorsed the *teachings* of Augustine, Dittes himself endorses Augustine's introspective and experiential *method*. This point is demonstrated aptly by quoting from a syllabus of Dittes, which Elledge reproduced in his essay on Dittes. The syllabus contained a two-pronged rationale for the inclusion of Augustine in a course on the theologies of Freud and Jung:

> (1) Augustine provides an appealing model for taking personal experience as a basis for theologizing: he offers unabashed introspection as a mode of theological reflection. He defines the theological enterprise, like life itself, as a dynamic process, a search. "Our heart is restless until it finds its rest in Thee," he wrote in his opening paragraph. What is the "restlessness" is a fundamental question to be asked of everyone, and what is the "rest"? (2) Augustine's theology provides a comparative reference point. *His* "restlessness"—focusing on guilt and struggles to trust—and *his* resolution—identifying a God reliable and benign enough to warrant a yielding trust—become a standard which both Freud and Jung were self-consciously resisting. I suspect most of us are somehow part of that same resistance movement.[84]

Dittes, as I have tried to show, *is* a part of this resistance movement.

CONCLUSION: RECALLING RELIGION

As noted in the conclusion of the previous chapter, in this book I am interested in what I am broadly calling reversals and restorations of religion. Each of my subjects reverse and restore religion in their own way and in doing so use their own language. I suggest that the language that seems most appropriate for Dittes in this regard is recalling religion. This suggestion is supported by the fact that Capps edited a volume of Dittes's writings titled *Re-Calling Ministry*.[85] In the forward to the volume, Peggy Way points out that the use of the word recalling in the title intimates not a looking backward but rather a summoning anew. If Dittes's writings on ministry as a whole can be captured with the word recalling—*Re-Calling Ministry* attempts to convey the essence of his ministerial writings—it is clear that

84. Elledge, "The Professor and the Saint," 177.

85. Dittes, *Re-Calling Ministry*.

Dittes never abandoned religion altogether; this is why I employed the notion of adaptive melancholia to understand the role of loss in Dittes's religious and vocational life. So the word choice of recalling fits with what I am calling a restoration of religion in that religion for Dittes, rather than being relinquished and subsequently mourned, is summoned anew.

However, as I have also tried to show in this chapter, Dittes was not entirely comfortable with religion—or, to put it another way, he did not accept uncritically the religion handed to him by tradition (cf. Galatians 1:9). I demonstrated this by focusing on Dittes's psychological portraits of Augustine and pointed out that they are subversive in the sense that Dittes endorses Augustine's theological method (introspection) but not his doctrinal conclusions (orthodoxy). This fits with what I am calling a reversal of religion.

In terms of the mourning religion thesis, what did writing about Augustine do for Dittes? What, psychologically and emotionally, was accomplished? I suggest that "Continuities between the Life and Thought of Augustine" (published in 1965), which focused on Augustine's journey through young adulthood and his relationship to his mother, helped Dittes to address *issues of commitment and identity*—especially those involving family and vocation. Dittes fathered four children between 1953 and 1958 (thus he committed to being a father), and during the 1960s he turned away from laboratory research to humanities-based inquiry (thus he committed to a radically different way of doing scholarship). So Dittes, when he was about to turn forty, decided to write about Augustine's *Confessions*—a book, perhaps not incidentally, that Augustine wrote when he was in his forties—and his analysis of Augustine's *Confessions* focused on issues of family and vocation in Augustine's life: what does it mean to be a man, Dittes asked of Augustine, and how does one separate from one's family of origin? Dittes saw his own life in Augustine in that Dittes was asking himself these questions as he was coming near the end of a decade-long process of making choices that set the direction for the rest of his life, choices that necessarily involved giving up other possibilities. These choices, which can be viewed as a kind of loss (but also gain), can be understood in light of stage one of Homans's theory. The death of his only son, Larry, in 1959 was also a major loss during this period.

I also suggest that "Augustine: The Search for a Fail-Safe God to Trust" (published in 1986), which focused on Augustine's solution to the religious dilemma regarding the soul's need for something sure or "fail-safe," helped Dittes to address *issues of over-commitment and relationality*—especially those involving divorce and remarriage. Between the years 1983 and 1987, Dittes divorced twice and remarried twice (he found himself over-committed to two relationships that just did not work out). So Dittes, when he was sixty, returned to the study of Augustine, perhaps also in search of something sure or "fail-safe" in his relational life, though he came to reject Augustine's solution (distance that yields stability) and instead endorsed risk (assurance is in the breaking). As Dittes earlier put it in *Minister on the Spot*: "One [should move] freely into risks and crises because [one] knows that in—and perhaps only in—crisis and disaster is there prospect of new revelation and new creation and new relation."[86] I suggest that Dittes's divorces and marriages also can be understood in light of stage one of Homans's theory. Additionally, the death of his mother a little later in 1993 was another major loss (which he may have experienced, in part, as a liberation), as well as his diagnosis of Parkinson's disease in 1994.

So what I am suggesting, in terms of the mourning religion thesis, is that the personal losses (e.g., the issues of commitment and over-commitment noted above) that Dittes faced constitute stage one of Homans's theory and the writing of the two essays on Augustine are reflective of stage two of Homans's theory (individuation from loss) because Dittes was working through his losses by working on Augustine. It is worth noting that the losses here do not entail becoming disabused with a particular religious teaching such as the failed prophecy discussed in the previous chapter (the stages do not fit so neatly with the case of Dittes, which is why I employed Cohler's notion of adaptive melancholia); the losses here are experiential rather than doctrinal but were religious in the sense that they challenged his personal sense of destiny.

What about stage three of Homans's theory: creation of meaning? I suggest that two books that Dittes published in 1996 are reflective of stage three—namely, *Driven by Hope* and *Men at Work*—because in these books Dittes redeems men by recalling the various commitments and over-commitments that men so often engender with regard to vocation and family, work and love. This new way of conceiving of men—and of conceiving of himself—came after he had constructed a psychological portrait of Augustine in the form of two essays. These essays enabled Dittes to find a saint who gave Dittes permission to mature into a restless boyhood in which

86. Dittes, *Minister on the Spot*, 100.

truth about God and self are not discerned by means of timeless doctrines but by starting afresh. This man, born on the day after Christmas who lived in the shadows of a chronic sense of destiny, invites us to do the same: to recall religion by planting and tending our own seeds in order to know God and ourselves because such knowledge requires—not permits, but *requires*—starting afresh.

4

Recovering Religion

> [S]ome areas of culture are more instructive for self-understanding than others. The most informative for me has been religion, including theology but also, and even more profoundly, spirituality, *because* it transcends intellectuality.[1]
>
> —William Bouwsma

INTRODUCTION

William James Bouwsma (1923–2004), Sather Professor of History at the University of California at Berkeley, was born to Oets Kolk "O. K." and Gertrude Bouwsma in Ann Arbor, Michigan, on November 22, 1923. He was born on his father's birthday. His younger brother Charles was born two years later, almost to the day, and his younger sister Gretchen was roughly ten years younger than Bouwsma. Bouwsma grew up in Lincoln, Nebraska. He married Beverly Hancock in 1944 at the age of twenty and they had four children: John, Sarah, Philip, and Paul. From 1943–1946 he served in the Air Force.

Bouwsma did his undergraduate and graduate work at Harvard University, receiving a BA in 1943 and a PhD in 1950. He referred to himself as a cultural historian. His specialty was on the Renaissance and the Reformation. Before retiring in 1991, Bouwsma taught at the University of Illinois

1. Bouwsma, "Introduction," 2.

Champaign-Urbana, Harvard University, and the University of California at Berkeley. He made the move to Berkeley in 1956 as a Visiting Professor and was promoted to Associate Professor in 1957. He taught at Berkeley for thirty some years, and served as Chair of the Department of History during the 1966–1967 academic year as well as from 1981 to 1983. And he served as Vice Chancellor for Academic Affairs from 1967 to 1969, during the student protests at Berkeley during the Vietnam War. He taught at Harvard for two years after his leadership as Vice Chancellor but returned to Berkeley after two years because he preferred Berkeley to Harvard (and Berkeley offered him an endowed chair to return). Bouwsma also served as the President for the American Historical Association in 1978.[2]

This chapter will have three parts. Part one will present Bouwsma's portrait of John Calvin. Part two will present personal information about Bouwsma from two academic essays. And part three will relate the life and work of Bouwsma in light of the mourning religion thesis. I have obtained biographical information about Bouwsma from personal disclosures in his books and articles, correspondence with his family and colleagues, and published interviews.

PART ONE: BOUWSMA'S HISTORICAL PORTRAIT OF CALVIN

Bouwsma's portrait of Calvin is divided into five parts with fourteen chapters plus an introduction and a conclusion. Part one, "The Man and the Times," places Calvin in his historical context. Part two, "The Labyrinth," deals with Calvin's desire for order. Part three, "The Opening," focuses on humanism. Part four, "The Abyss," has chapters on being, knowing, power, and drama. The final section, "A Program for the Times," offers Calvin's take on society, polity, and church. In the introduction (subtitled "The Quest for the Historical Calvin," a seeming reference to Albert Schweitzer's *The Quest of the Historical Jesus*[3]), Bouwsma notes that he is offering a *portrait*, not a biography, of Calvin because the basic facts of Calvin's life are well known and such an approach enables him to convey the essence of Calvin's personality. This book is, Bouwsma writes, "not simply a portrait; it is a *sixteenth-century* portrait. I am less interested in Calvin's inner life for its own sake than in using it to illuminate the momentous cultural crisis

2. Lage, "Bouwsma," xvii, 1, 11–14, 18–27.

3. Schweitzer, *The Quest*.

central to his century."[4] Bouwsma understands Calvin as in dialogue with various antithetical impulses of the sixteenth century and in himself and as a man who could only achieve partial and limited success in balancing—*not* reconciling—these impulses.

The Man and the Times

A Sixteenth Century Life

In chapter 1, Bouwsma offers a brief overview of Calvin's life. Calvin was born in Noyon, France, on July 10, 1509, and he was the youngest of four or five children, all of whom were boys. His mother died a few years after his birth; Calvin was subsequently sent to live with another family. His father remarried shortly after his wife's death.

Calvin's father wanted him to become a priest and so sent him to the University of Paris when he was twelve. Calvin finished his degree, but, when he was about twenty, his father decided that he should become a lawyer instead. As an obedient son, Calvin began to work on his law degree. Along the way, Calvin maintained an interest in humanism and even published a commentary on an essay by Seneca a year after his father's death in 1531. Regarding these events, Bouwsma observes that

> [t]he death of his mother when he was a small child and his subsequent exclusion from his father's household may have begun in him a sense of homelessness that would be later deepened by exile; he grieved for his motherland all his life. The loss of mother and home may also have been an element in what seemed to me his undeniably ambiguous feelings about his father.[5]

Bouwsma adds that Calvin never spoke warmly about his father.

Calvin received a humanistic education in Paris, learning Latin, Hebrew, Greek, and Erasmianist teachings. In 1533 Calvin fled Paris after his friend, Nicolas Cop, preached a controversial sermon. He fled because, Bouwsma suggests, Calvin likely collaborated with Cop in the writing of the sermon. If not quite heretical by Roman Catholic standards—Cop criticized the notion that good works can pave the way to eternal life—the sermon at least threatened the peace and so Calvin eventually followed Cop to Basel. For the rest of his life, Calvin lived as somewhat of an exile. In 1535

4. Bouwsma, *Calvin*, 4.

5. Ibid., 11.

Calvin was still unsure what to do with his life, but he began to write seriously then, and he finished the first edition of the *Institutes of the Christian Religion* by the end of the summer.

Bouwsma notes that Guillaume Farel, the leader of the Genevan Reformation, became Calvin's mentor. As Calvin tells the story about their relationship, he had only intended a short stay in Geneva but Farel forced him, against his wishes, to remain. In 1538, however, Calvin and Farel were expelled from Geneva. They first went to Basel, and Calvin then went to Strasbourg. In Strasbourg, Martin Bucer became Calvin's new mentor. The situation was much more stable there for Calvin, and he was able to attend to both his scholarly and pastoral inclinations. It was here that he wrote some of his most influential writings, such as his commentary on Romans and his reply to Cardinal Sadoleto. He also expanded and revised the *Institutes*.

Bucer took responsibility for finding Calvin a wife. In 1540, he married Idelette de Bure, a widow with two children. They had three children together but none survived infancy. While he had no biological children of his own, Calvin bragged that he had ten thousand spiritual children. De Bure died in 1549, leaving Calvin distraught. He never remarried.

The possibility of returning to Geneva presented itself—there was a group in Geneva working to return exiled pastors—but Calvin was reluctant to do so. When he was formally invited back, he sought the council of Bucer, who told him to return. And so on September 2, 1541, he did. Calvin was more mature when he returned; he also was more cautious as well as more assertive, as he demanded that the town live "in accordance with the principle that 'the church cannot stand firm unless a government is constituted as prescribed to us by the Word of God and observed in the early church.'"[6] The town council conceded his wishes by endorsing his *Ecclesiastical Ordinances*. Bouwsma offers a psychological interpretation of what this might have meant for Calvin:

> There was probably a personal element in Calvin's concern to order Geneva. A righteous community administered by city "fathers" would be a good father writ large. At the same time, as a *home*, nurturing as well as ordering and protecting, it might represent the mother he could scarcely remember. Exile could also

6. Ibid., 24.

> be justified by the creation in another place of something better than—and therefore a reproach to—what he had left behind.[7]

Bouwsma notes that Calvin spent most of his time on his commentaries when he returned to Geneva and that he also spent a great deal of time on his pastoral duties, preaching some 4,000 sermons and, in the decade after 1550, undertaking about 270 weddings and 50 baptisms.

Calvin died on May 27, 1564. He had a number of medical problems: "His ailments included, by his own account, arthritis, kidney stones, unspecified intestinal disorders, hemorrhoids, bleeding from the stomach, fever, muscle cramps, nephritis [a severe inflation of the kidney], and gout."[8] "But," Bouwsma writes, "it is possible that the tensions and conflicts within himself were even more erosive: notably, as this account of his life may already have hinted, the tension between the trust that he had found in Cop's address of 1534 and the insecurity that was both hidden and revealed in his need to control himself and his environment."[9]

Calvin's Anxiety

Bouwsma's focus on Calvin's anxiety is the key distinguishing feature of his portrait. Chapter 2 provides a general overview of Calvin's anxiety. "I am in danger of being unjust to God's mercy," Calvin wrote, "by laboring with so much anxiety to assert it, as if it were doubtful or obscure."[10] Bouwsma observes a wide vocabulary of anxiety throughout Calvin's discourse: *anxietas, solicitude, angoisse, destresse, frayeur*, and *perplexité*. And Calvin used all of these words to write about his many anxieties. He wondered, for example, about the natural order of the world. Storms made him anxious. He associated sin with disorder, pollution, and mixture. He was anxious about the body, especially his own: "Our body is the receptacle of a thousand diseases."[11] Life is uncertain, and anxiety universal: "But for every human being," Bouwsma writes, "beyond the future, beyond the limits of time, lurk the uncertainties surrounding death; this is why, in some ultimate sense,

7. Ibid., 25.
8. Ibid., 30–31.
9. Ibid., 31.
10. Ibid., 32.
11. Ibid., 40.

all anxiety is about death."[12] But Calvin also thought that anxiety was part of creation, as "the mother of prudence," and that the theological virtue of hope depended on anxiety in that anxiety prepared one's heart for the Gospel.

How did Calvin deal with anxiety? "The alternatives open to Calvin in coping with anxiety, both his own and that of his age, are," Bouwsma writes, "suggested by two of his favorite images for describing situations of extreme spiritual discomfort. The images are of an abyss . . . and a labyrinth."[13] Bouwsma notes that the term "abyss" has had a long history in western discourse. For the Greeks it had such meanings as meaninglessness and non-being, while for the Latin Fathers it meant hell (though later Fathers also interpreted it positively, noting that the infinity of God is like an abyss). Calvin was aware of all of these meanings. The term "labyrinth" also was used to express and to induce certain experiences, such as "the powerlessness of human beings to extricate themselves from a self-centered alienation from God."[14] Bouwsma writes, "The Latin root of *anxietas—angustia*, literally the sensation of being compressed and suffocated—hints at what Calvin was trying to convey by 'labyrinth.'"[15] So "Calvin associated anxiety, then, with two rather different, indeed almost diametrically opposed sensations: with a kind of vertigo and disorientation in which his own identity and sense of direction were endangered, but also with a feeling that the whole of reality was pressing in on him from all directions, crushing out his life and breath."[16] But, as Bouwsma notes, "Calvin seems to me to have been more disturbed, and at a deeper level, by the abyss than by the labyrinth."[17] This observation that there were at least two kinds of anxiety in Calvin ultimately led Bouwsma to suggest that there were "psychologically and culturally not one but (at least) two Calvins."[18] The rest of the book is dedicated to exploring these two Calvins.

12. Ibid.
13. Ibid., 45.
14. Ibid., 46.
15. Ibid., 47.
16. Ibid.
17. Ibid., 48.
18. Ibid., 33.

A World Out of Joint

In chapter 3, Bouwsma suggests that Europeans during the later Middle Ages were becoming increasingly sensitive to the failings of their world and, therefore, more anxious. Calvin's severe moralism, Bouwsma asserts, signaled the intensity of his anxiety. Bouwsma observes this anxious moralism in a wide range of areas that he wanted to control. Calvin looked around and saw much to attack: widespread sins associated with unrestraint (e.g., greed, gluttony, lust, drunkenness) as well as common groups of people prone to sinning (e.g., the powerful, the rich, women). "The world," Bouwsma writes, "was indeed in a deplorable condition, but the grimmest element in its plight was, for Calvin, the state of the church."[19] The church was "a den of thieves" and "disordered." The church had become greedy, and it, too, had lusted after power. Ancient popes and recent ones disturbed Calvin, and he lamented the state of his beloved France (France had become "contaminated" by outsiders). Princes no longer ruled for the people, alms were not given from the heart, young people no longer respected their elders, rapes and adulteries were frequent, and, perhaps worst of all, religious ignorance and unbelief were more widespread than ever. "But what gave Calvin particular cause for anxiety," Bouwsma writes, "was the imminence of divine punishment far more serious than anything the world had yet experienced. For human beings were not repenting of their sins."[20] Bouwsma concludes: "Clearly, for Calvin, there was much to be anxious about: enough, certainly, to propel even this reclusive intellectual into the active life."[21]

The Labyrinth

Cosmic Inheritances

In chapter 4, Bouwsma begins by noting that the crisis in western civilization known as the Renaissance included a growing awareness of the tensions between Hellenic and Hebraic influences within itself; he also notes that Calvin, in face of this cultural crisis, "clung to traditional certainties because he preferred the familiar dangers of the labyrinth to an abyss of

19. Ibid., 59.
20. Ibid., 65.
21. Ibid.

doubt."[22] Bouwsma argues that traditional culture was absolutist, authoritarian, and optimistic. Reality in traditional culture was something to be passively perceived and such knowledge was equated with seeing, though there was no or little awareness of perspective. Epistemologically, differences of opinion were considered a matter of incomplete knowledge and/or perversity. Theologically, traditional culture:

> reinforced the belief that human beings can know God as he is, unhampered by the limitations of the human condition; and it implied that theology is a science, devised by God and communicated in his books of nature and Scripture, that presents truths from his perspective. For this reason human knowledge, and notably theological knowledge, can claim a *certitude* that reflects its divine origin.[23]

The order of the cosmos provided Calvin some comfort and also influenced his notion of calling; just as each heavenly body has its own established orbit so, too, do human beings in society. Calvin believed that society is, or should be, structured by the family, polity, and the church. If Calvin had a fairly clear notion of how he believed society should be structured, he struggled over how human beings were structured internally (or psychologically) and was inconsistent and confused about his theological anthropology. What *is* clear, though, is how his doctrine of total depravity affects human beings: Sin affects the whole human being—mind, body, soul, spirit, will, intellect, desire.

A word here about Calvin's view of history is also in order: It is one of general decline but also includes a notion of cycles because, from time to time, things get so bad that a spirit of reform is born. Thinking about the cosmos comforted Calvin and helped him deal with his anxiety to a certain extent because renewal and rebirth, as the seasons attest, is possible.

Restoring Order

In chapter 5, Bouwsma observes that Calvin believed that the order of the world depended on the control of the lower faculties by the higher faculties: Children should be controlled by parents, women by men, men by civil and religious leaders, and everyone by God. Calvin also believed that

22. Ibid., 69.

23. Ibid., 71.

moderation—one of the ancient virtues—was the foundation of order. Calvin thought that there were a number of ways to restore order to the world, and, as a typical humanist of his time, he believed that education could create better citizens. Human beings, by the grace of God, do have some ability to reform themselves. He also believed that individual efforts to reform could be aided by public opinion, shame, private admonition, and guilt. Other ways of inculcating virtue included the teaching of history, inspiring the fear of punishment, encouraging the imitation of Christ, and biblical exegesis. While the world was out of joint, it could be put back together—and he was anxious to do so.

Rational Religion

The subject of chapter 6 is Calvin's Christianity, which was, above all else, an *intellectual* form of Christianity: "there is no faith where there is no knowledge," Calvin asserted.[24] He believed that true religion was clear, free of ambiguity, and rational. In seeking to put together an orderly religion, Calvin came to hold a number of interesting intellectual and theological positions. While, for example, he did not deny that Scripture is rich and inexhaustible in terms of wisdom, he did deny the possibility of multiple meanings. He was attracted to natural theology. Calvin asserted the doctrines of God's immutability and impassibility but also struggled to make complete sense of the Bible in this regard (he denied, for example, that God felt anger or grief but could not bring himself to suggest that God did not love). While Calvin believed that human beings are made in the image of God, he nevertheless maintained his doctrine of total depravity. "[I]n spite of his effort to make sense of the universe and to tie it all together in a single tidy package, Bouwsma writes, "Calvin remained anxious."[25] He continues: "Indeed, the more he articulated his orderly universe, the more he worried over the permeability of boundaries, the collapse of categories, contamination and impurity; and the more he felt trapped. He could move, for relief, only in the opposite direction, toward freedom."[26]

24. Ibid., 100.
25. Ibid., 109.
26. Ibid.

The Opening: Humanism

In chapter 7, Bouwsma offers an interpretation of Calvin that is less rigid than is often presented. His presentation is based on the observation that Calvin's humanism led Calvin to mitigate the claustrophobic effects of his commitments to traditional culture by, for example, enabling him to see that there were errors in the copying of the New Testament; that different interpretations of Scripture are possible; and that the biblical authors occasionally made factual mistakes (e.g., he corrected Matthew 2:9–10 on the issue of a star guiding the magi in the story of the birth of Jesus—Calvin thought that it was a comet). His humanism also enabled him to disagree with Paul on matters of culture. And he also noted that the Gospel accounts do not agree on particular details, and to ignore these facts is, Calvin thought, ignorance pure and simple.

A key point in this chapter involves Calvin's commitment to decorum, which, for humanists, means that messages need to be tailored to the audience. So-called "mistakes" in the Bible do not discredit the Word of God but rather demonstrate that God speaks to us in ways that we need to hear. This means that "Calvin's sensitivity to 'differences of time' implied that what is right for one age in the history of the church might be rejected by another."[27] Theology, then, is not a timeless system that is done once and for all but is, rather, something that has to be constantly rewritten. This more flexible Calvin was not as subject to the anxieties of disorder. Yet he had something else to be anxious about: the abyss of freedom.

The Abyss

Being

In chapter 8, Bouwsma focuses on Calvin's ideas regarding what it means to be a human being. As noted, Calvin was not able to articulate a completely consistent and coherent conception. At times he praised feelings and the body—affirming the pleasures of wine and sex—so long as one was not driven to excess. He rejected asceticism. Sometimes Calvin was sexist; other times he was more egalitarian. Bouwsma notes that Calvin talks negatively about human beings with regard to sin (e.g., even our minds are affected by sin) so frequently that some have argued that Calvin did not believe that

27. Ibid., 124.

human beings still have the image of God inside of them. But Bouwsma points out that this is a misunderstanding of Calvin. Indeed, in other passages in Calvin—passages that are not dealing with sin—one can observe clearly that Calvin believes that human beings still retain the image of God.

It is striking that Calvin's understanding of original sin paved the way for notions of progress.[28] Calvin attacked tradition, custom, and the veneration of the ancients—both pagan and Christian—and he lamented with other humanists the fact that Rome regressed from a republic to a monarchy and that religion, too, declined in the empire. In the church, he saw the medieval fathers as building on the mistakes of the ancient fathers. Bouwsma notes that Calvin had little respect for old age because he thought that *all* of the stages of life were dismal. According to Calvin, things were *not* better in the old days; nor were our fathers more virtuous than we. They were just as sinful as we are, but we have a chance to set things right.

Knowing

In chapter 9, Bouwsma focuses on the problem of knowledge for Calvin. While Calvin rejected the traditional sovereignty of reason on the grounds that human beings were both more *and* less than intellectual, he believed that certainty depends on God's grace and that the mind does not have the powers it once did before the Fall: "In the absence of divine revelation," Bouwsma writes, "Calvin recommended, on religious matters, a deliberate agnosticism."[29] Calvin also believed, in accord with other humanists, that knowledge must be *useful*. Also, he denounced curiosity. And he preferred passive ways of knowing. While Calvin insisted that God is rational, he also held that God's rationality is not human rationality. Based upon this line of reasoning, Calvin could conclude that there is justice and order in the world even if it appears that this is not so. So, theology for Calvin, though a thoroughly human enterprise, is a viable and serious intellectual project because through theology one seeks to discern, to a limited extent and by means of God's grace, knowledge of God and ourselves.

28. Troeltsch, *Protestantism and Progress*. Also see Kuyper, *Lectures on Calvinism*.

29. Bouwsma, *Calvin*, 155.

Power

Just as anxiety pervaded Calvin's discourse so, too, did power: "Because it expressed his sense of powerlessness to control the future," Bouwsma writes, "his anxiety was itself closely related to his preoccupation with power."[30] In chapter 10, Bouwsma focuses on the fact that, for Calvin, God's power was infinite and that key metaphors for him included the power of the weather and of rulers. He especially liked metaphors involving weather (e.g., thunder), as they implied God's direct power in the world.

In Calvin's view, God's power extends over all of life and death. Bouwsma argued that, with regard to Calvin's doctrine of providence, "[w]hat is indisputable is the importance Calvin attached to the doctrine for the relief of anxiety" and that "[i]t comforted him to reflect [on the fact] that the power of God holds the universe in place, preserves its order, prevents it from sliding into the abyss."[31] Relatedly, the doctrine of predestination, Bouwsma argues, was for Calvin (1) biblical; (2) a logical and necessary corollary of God's power; and (3) confirmed experientially in our own lives because, while many people hear the Gospel, not all come to believe. Additionally, Bouwsma also points out that the doctrine of predestination can only be understood within the life of faith and in the context of the doctrine of salvation.

Drama

In chapter 11, Bouwsma observes that the sixteenth century was one of the great periods in the history of the theater and that theater during this period expressed the uncertainties of a time of rapid change in which the possibilities of human existence were radically expanding.[32] Calvin described the world as "a glorious theater" in which human beings admired God's works and at other times performed the role of actors. As one might suspect, however, Calvin was uncomfortable with the notion of "play" because he worried about the implication that, when one is acting, one is in a sense being disingenuous or inauthentic in that one is playing a role. But he also believed that playing the role of a repentant sinner actually encouraged genuine repentance. Calvin's notion of "calling" also fits with his vision of

30. Ibid., 162.

31. Ibid., 171.

32. On this point, see Greenblatt, *Hamlet in Purgatory*.

the drama of the Christian life in that just as actors are assigned roles so also does God assign various roles or callings to different persons.

Calvin tells the story of the Christian life according to two plots. One plot centers on struggle, the other on pilgrimage. Bouwsma writes: "Just as the militant Christian can depend, with God's help, on victory, so the Christian pilgrim can be sure that, however slowly, he will reach his goal."[33] Implied in both of Calvin's metaphors for the Christian life—the soldier and the pilgrim—is the notion of progress. While Calvin was comforted by the fact that, with God's help, the elect are guaranteed of reaching the goal, he was nevertheless anxious about the idea of progress because, for him, it was a *duty*.

A Program for the Times

Society

In chapter 12, Bouwsma explores Calvin's belief that he was called to confront the moral and spiritual crises of his time. Calvin conceived of God as *legislateur et roy* (God governs us), and part of God's governance includes restoring the world to order through the institution of social traditions and structures (which included secular institutions). Bouwsma notes that Calvin accepted existing social distinctions but did not admire them. Regarding economic class, Calvin believed that poorer individuals had closer families, were more hospitable, and were freer from envy. Yet Calvin also defended wealth so long as it was used for the glorification of God. He also believed that private property was central to social order. So, for Calvin, poverty was not a virtue but neither was extreme wealth—wealth ought to be used for the collective good. He upheld prudence and frugality (both with regard to money and time), and the basis for human society ought to be the Golden Rule as applied to the needs of human community.

Polity

In chapter 13, Bouwsma notes that Calvin made a distinction between political authority and religious authority, and held that *all* authority comes from God. This means that civil authority, for Calvin, is a calling. He thought that clergy should not do the tasks of princes and princes should not do the

33. Bouwsma, *Calvin*, 186.

tasks of clergy. According to Calvin, it is the duty of Christians to obey their rulers, even wicked rulers. In cases of tyranny, Calvin still discourages active rebellion but does permit passive disobedience, such as not obeying a tyrant's command to do something wicked. The form of government that Calvin advocated was the republic (because monarchs can easily become tyrants), as he believed that liberty is necessary for the achievement of full humanity.

Church

In chapter 14, Bouwsma notes that Calvin believed that the improvement of society depends on the improvement of individuals and that the means of transforming individuals lay within the church. Calvin believed that the unity of the church was spiritual, that church attendance was necessary, and that individuals should not be free to read the Bible on their own in an attempt to discover what it means (yet he also held that God speaks to individuals). Calvin attempted to transform Geneva into a visible community of saints and used excommunication as a means to keep the church pure. While Calvin was deeply authoritarian in matters of church order, at times he could be flexible, which is reflected in his belief that nothing is binding except what is plainly spelled out in Scripture.

Conclusion

Bouwsma concludes his book with a discussion of Montaigne. He notes Montaigne's comment that

> [I]t has often seemed to me that even good authors are wrong to insist on fashioning a consistent and solid fabric out of us. They choose one general characteristic and go and arrange and interpret all a man's actions to fit their picture.[34]

Bouwsma believes that he has avoided the charge of reductionism by offering "two Calvins." One Calvin was philosophical and rational. This is the Calvin who craved order and certainty, distrusted freedom and the world, and sought to control the forces both in himself and in the world. Bouwsma's metaphor for this Calvin was "the labyrinth." The other Calvin was rhetorical and humanistic and valued experience over theory and was

34. Ibid., 230.

generally more flexible and tolerant. Bouwsma's metaphor for this Calvin was "the abyss." "In Calvin's struggle to *reduce* the incompatible impulses in himself to a comfortable integrity," Bouwsma writes, "his philosophical side was more dominant, seeking to reconcile and unite them dialectically."[35] Calvinism—that is, Calvin's own Calvinism—was a composite: "[i]t was the product of impulses and needs of varying provenance that defied systematization."[36] This anxious Calvin, Bouwsma concludes, who was both medieval and modern, both philosophical and rhetorical, can teach us much about our collective past.

PART TWO: INSIGHTS ABOUT BOUWSMA'S LIFE FROM HIS WORK—TWO ESSAYS

My approach in this chapter is a little different from my previous chapters. This is because Capps published many books and articles containing a great deal of autobiographical content, and Dittes, while not publishing as much, did the same. In contrast, Bouwsma did not publish as much autobiographical material. So this chapter is more inductive. In this section I draw on two essays, one of which is autobiographical and the other theological.

The Historian as Public Servant

In *A Usable Past*, a self-edited volume of his own works that he published a year before his retirement, Bouwsma writes autobiographically about his career. He dedicated the book to Jean and Henry May. Henry May, a long-time friend and colleague of Bouwsma's, "offered this assessment of Bouwsma's work: 'His historical thought was powerful, complex and profound. It was quarried, sometimes painfully, from sources that lay deep in his personality and experience.'"[37] In the introduction of *A Usable Past*, Bouwsma begins by noting that he took the book's title from Friedrich Nietzsche's "On the Uses and Disadvantages of History for Life." Bouwsma writes: "The central argument of this passionate work, judiciously qualified, reflects my own deepest convictions about the value of historical scholarship," that "a vital historiography must serve the 'life and action' of society," and that

35. Ibid., 231.

36. Ibid.

37. Brucker, "In Memoriam." My emphasis.

"[h]istory, in this view, much like water and electricity, is *a public utility*."[38] So if Bouwsma sees himself as a public servant, one may wonder what type of contribution he sees himself making to society—that is, what kind of public servant is he, what type of historian? In his early years, he thought of himself as an intellectual historian but, after the influence of historicism, he came to recognize that the conception of "the intellect" was itself "a historical artifact" and so began calling himself a cultural historian (he was particularly influenced by Mary Douglass, Clifford Geertz, and Marshall Sahlins for his understanding of culture). As a public servant, Bouwsma worked as a cultural historian to help manage the existential anxiety of society.

After noting what he had learned from some of his most influential teachers (such as Paul Kristeller and Douglass Bush), Bouwsma points out that he has always been more interested in tensions rather than harmonies in western culture and attributes this to the fact that he was the son of "second-generation Dutch Calvinist immigrants who were trying to assimilate the high culture of early-twentieth-century America," which, as he put it, "posed problems for me."[39] In addressing these problems, Bouwsma was particularly drawn to this line in Nietzsche: "Historical knowledge . . . streams in unceasingly from inexhaustible wells, the strange and incoherent forces its way forward, memory opens all its gates and yet is not open wide enough, nature struggles to receive, arrange and honor these strange guests, but they themselves are in conflict with one another and it seems necessary to constrain them and control them if one is not oneself to perish in their conflict."[40] Reflecting on this passage, Bouwsma writes, "[a]s I entered the world of scholarship on my own, I increasingly saw that my task as a historian would be to try to sort out the major elements in the heterogeneous bundle of impulses that constitute [w]estern culture and lay bare its contraries," and the "relief of the anxiety engendered by cultural conflict also figured more and more centrally in my project."[41] "A historian," Bouwsma continues, "might, by exposing contradictions arising out of the eclecticism of [w]estern culture, contribute to conscious and informed choice."[42]

38. Bouwsma, "Introduction," 1.

39. Ibid., 8.

40. Ibid.

41. Ibid.

42. Ibid., 8–9.

Christian Adulthood

Another essay in *A Useable Past* useful for my purposes is "Christian Adulthood."[43] This paper was given on a panel over which Erik Erikson presided and was later published in a special edition of *Daedalus*. Bouwsma begins his essay by noting that "the elasticity" of Christianity is well known and, therefore, poses problems for attempts to identify a peculiarly Christian conception of adulthood. He believes that such a conception can be made if one makes a distinction between historical and normative Christianity: historical Christianity "reflects the composite of those cultural impulses that make up what is commonly thought of as Christian civilization," while normative Christianity "is an ideal type."[44] By ideal type, he means that "it builds upon and is consistent with those biblical norms about human nature and human destiny that give to Christianity whatever precise identity it may possess."[45] He makes another distinction between manhood and adulthood. He notes that the Germanic word "man," which typically is gender specific, means "to think," and that the chief idea being expressed by manhood is to distinguish human beings from animals in that human beings can think in ways that animals cannot. The Latin word "adult" means "to grow up" and "implies a process rather than the possession of a particular status or specific faculty."[46] Bouwsma next goes on to assert his own conception of Christian adulthood and quotes Paul's letter to the Ephesians: "So shall we all at last attain to the unity inherent in our faith and our knowledge of the Son of God—to mature manhood, measured by nothing less than the full stature of Christ" (Ephesians 4:13).[47] "But," Bouwsma writes, "it is of particular importance for our immediate purposes that the measure of true adulthood is finally 'the full stature of Christ,' for this is an absolute standard, in relation to which no man, whatever his age, can claim to be fully an adult."[48] Next Bouwsma quotes Calvin: "After being born in Christ, we ought to grow, so as not to be children in understanding . . . although we have not arrived at man's estate, we are at any rate

43. Bouwsma notes that this is one of the few papers of his that his father read. He thinks that this is because this vision of Christianity is congruent with O. K.'s vision. See Lage, "Bouwsma," 43.

44. Bouwsma, "Christian Adulthood," 397.

45. Ibid., 398.

46. Ibid.

47. Ibid., 401.

48. Ibid., 402.

older boys."[49] Bouwsma concludes: "Christianity has, then, a conception of full adulthood; the goal of human development is total conformity to the manhood of Christ," and "[i]t is in this sense that the Christian life is like adolescence, that stage in which the adult seems, however ambiguously, trembling to be born."[50]

From here Bouwsma makes some interesting theological claims. He claims that the refusal to grow is the source of sin and, he thinks, that the Christian story of the Fall (Genesis 3) supports this claim. In other words, Adam and Eve are punished because they refuse to grow. However, the story actually seems to support the opposite view—namely, that Adam and Eve are punished precisely *because they want to grow* by means of eating from the Tree of Knowledge.[51] Yet Bouwsma reads Adam and Eve's sin as rooted in the fact that they wanted to be like gods, meaning that Adam and Eve wanted to remain as they were. This seems to be somewhat of an idiosyncratic reading. So, too, with his next theological claim: "The claim to divinity, therefore, paradoxically results in pervasive anxiety."[52] The fact that Adam and Eve experienced guilt and shame can be supported in the text—this has been observed for centuries—but why *anxiety*, and why *pervasive* anxiety? Moreover, with what kind of evidence could one support the claim that all human beings experience pervasive anxiety after the Fall? It occurs to me that one response here could involve the question of death. It is often assumed by Christians that death became a part of the human experience after the Fall, and, following this logic, pervasive anxiety could be seen as becoming a part of the human condition. But when one reads Genesis 1 through 3 closely, one finds that *death was always a part of God's creation*. Indeed, God forbids human beings from eating from the Tree of Knowledge because *then* they would know to eat from the Tree of Life (Genesis 3:22), suggesting that God apparently wants to prevent human beings from living forever because they would become like gods (being godlike seems to mean having knowledge and eternal life).[53] To be sure,

49. Ibid.

50. Ibid. This is in stark contrast to Dittes's notion of "maturing into boyhood."

51. See Pagels, *Adam, Eve, and the Serpent*. Also see Kripal, *The Serpent's Gift*.

52. Bouwsma, "Christian Adulthood," 406.

53. See Birch, Brueggemann, Fretheim, and Petersen, *A Theological Introduction to the Old Testament*, 51–52. They write: "The penalty for eating is death—capital punishment, not ontological change (from being immortal to being mortal), for death as such is part of God's created order. If this were not the case, the [T]ree of [L]ife would have been irrelevant."

Bouwsma is not entirely alone in his reading of the Fall; on this point he is in the majority. In fact, he notes that his interpretations of sin, anxiety, and the Fall have been derived from Paul Ricoeur and Reinhold Niebuhr. He also draws on other theologians such as Paul Tillich, Karl Barth, and Harvey Cox. Many of these thinkers (and others such as Rollo May) were writing about anxiety from the 1950s onward, and so this may explain Bouwsma's interest in reading pervasive anxiety into Genesis 3.

Bouwsma also writes about the meaning of salvation in a way that reminds one of Tillich's correlational method, where theology answers the questions of culture: "If," he writes, "the Christian analysis of evils in historical existence can be understood as a diagnosis of immaturity, the Christian conception of salvation can be similarly construed as a description of the only way to recover that capacity for growth in which true adulthood exists."[54] He continues, "The basic problem here is to replace anxiety with faith, so that man can enter an open future with confidence and grow through his experience."[55]

Bouwsma concludes his essay by making a case for both childhood and community. He suggests that childhood, like the Christian life, assumes growth, but childhood is good in its own right and has aspects worth retaining in adulthood. Children are open and filled with wonder and have a sense of playfulness. They can relax. They can take risks for the sake of some adventure. He quotes Zechariah 8:5 in support of his view of play: "And the streets of the city shall be full of boys and girls, playing in the streets."[56] Regarding community, Bouwsma notes that he has treated various elements of a Christian conception of adulthood as normative for individual development but adds that to ignore the communal aspects of growth would betray the Christian tradition because Paul's words about growth and maturity were intended for a community of believers.

A Useable Faith

These two essays, while interesting in their own right, provide us with valuable information about Bouwsma as a person. We learn from his introduction in *A Usable Past* that (1) Bouwsma views the discipline of history as a vocation in that the historian is a "public servant" and that the way in which

54. Bouwsma, "Christian Adulthood," 407.

55. Ibid., 408.

56. Ibid., 412.

historians carry out this vocation is by making it "usable"; (2) Bouwsma, as a cultural historian, saw it as his personal task to address cultural anxiety; and (3) Bouwsma indicates that he has addressed his own personal needs by making the past usable for himself.

His essay on Christian adulthood is also instructive for understanding Bouwsma as a person, though in a less direct way, as it gives us insight into his faith life. Bouwsma makes four main theological claims in this essay: (1) there is a difference between historical and normative Christianity; (2) Christian adulthood is growing toward conformity to Christ; (3) complete conformity to Christ is not possible in this life; and (4) the refusal to grow is sin, which results in pervasive anxiety. What we have here is not an "objective" (if objectivity is possible or desirable[57]) or even a historical account of various Christian conceptions of adulthood—what one might expect from a historian—but rather a normative and theological argument. And all such arguments tell us as much about the person making the argument as they do about whatever topic the author happens to be advocating because all theological statements are personal. Taken together, Bouwsma's four theological statements suggest that the task of the Christian, at bottom, is growth, and that Christians should not be anxious about the future but should approach the future with openness and faith—this, it seems, is the core of Bouwsma's personal faith.

PART THREE: APPLYING THE MOURNING RELIGION THESIS

How did Bouwsma get to his usable faith? I now turn to the application of the mourning religion thesis to seek an explanation. In doing so, I present biographical material about Bouwsma and, toward the end of this section, demonstrate how Bouwsma's personal experiences influenced his portrait of Calvin.

Bouwsma, Sarah Bouwsma explained to me, "was so cautious in what he said. We all knew he suffered from his relationship with his own father, never getting the approval he wanted."[58] Bouwsma turned to the psychological study of Calvin shortly after the death of his father in 1978. I argue that Bouwsma's psychological portrait of Calvin helped Bouwsma to individuate from his father by recovering a humanist Calvin who was much

57. See Novick, *That Noble Dream*.

58. Personal Correspondence, May 20, 2008.

more human and humane than the Calvin of Dutch Calvinism, a more flexible Calvin who would give Bouwsma approval and, therefore, some relief from anxiety. In making this case, I begin by presenting biographical information about Bouwsma's father.

The Context of Loss

In *Something about O. K. Bouwsma*, Ronald Hustwit, one of O. K.'s former graduate students, recounts his experiences with O. K.[59] Hustwit undertook this project about ten years after O. K.'s death and, when writing the account, drew on not only his twenty-five year relationship with O. K. but also the Bouwsma family. My presentation of O. K. will be based, to a great extent, on Hustwit's portrait.

O. K. was born in Muskegon, Michigan, in 1898. His parents, Dutch-Americans, had close ties to both Holland and to various Dutch-American communities in Michigan. O. K. went to Calvin College for his undergraduate education and the University of Michigan for his graduate education. In 1928, he took a teaching position at the University of Nebraska, where he taught until his retirement in 1965. Nebraska at the time had a mandatory retirement at the age of 65. After his retirement, he taught for twelve more years at the University of Texas in Austin, Texas. O. K. was interested in Georg Hegel and idealism in his early career, but he gradually became more interested in Ludwig Wittgenstein—with whom O. K. was a personal friend—as well as Søren Kierkegaard. His reading of Kierkegaard and others, Hustwit suggests, "gave [O. K.] guidance on understanding the central force in his life—his Christian faith."[60]

Hustwit first heard of O. K. at Westminster College in New Wilmington, Pennsylvania. At Westminster, Jack Rogers encouraged him to pursue his interests in Christian philosophy with O. K. at the University of Nebraska. Rogers told Hustwit about O. K.'s "persistence in asking for examples and specific cases in response to generalizations" and "quick wit in philosophical discussions."[61] Hustwit also recalled a story that Rogers had told him about O. K. during his senior year at Westminster. Rogers had just returned from a conference on Christian philosophy, and he mentioned to Hustwit that one presenter was trying to draw implications from Thomas

59. Huswit, *Something about O. K. Bouwsma*.

60. Ibid., ix.

61. Ibid., 1.

Aquinas's proof based on degrees of perfection in art and O. K., apparently unimpressed, sarcastically asked "some questions about whether one of [Ludwig van] Beethoven's symphonies was a more perfect creation than some current Elvis Presley tune."[62] The audience laughed and O. K. continued poking fun at the Thomist by concluding his remarks with the exclamation, "God exists!" Rogers recalls that the presenter then tried to address some of O. K.'s comments and asked, "What would you say if a voice came to you in the middle of the night claiming: 'I am the most perfect being greater than which nothing can be conceived'?"[63] "Congratulations," O. K. responded. The presenter, apparently irritated at this point, said: "Professor Bouwsma we are waiting for you to say more," but O. K. would not engage the presenter any further.[64] After hearing such stories, Hustwit "wanted to meet this person who dared enter into the arena of philosophical warfare armed with humor alone and who was apparently fearless."[65]

O. K. Bouwsma as a Frustrating Teacher

In a seminar with O. K., Hustwit noted that O. K. would not allow a piece of philosophical terminology go by without challenge. He added that O. K. sometimes asked students to write what they had just said on the board, and then the class would focus on the "offending sentence," which was often frustrating:

> One sometimes had the feeling that he was deliberately being obtusive. "Others may be talking nonsense, but I am not," one might think to oneself. Or one might feel that if he would only let me finish, he could explain all this to [O. K.]'s satisfaction. Some too felt that he was not taking them seriously when they were speaking of philosophical matters of great significance to them. Another might be upset over the fact that the argument that he had put forward and had been received so badly was none other than one put forward by some great philosopher in the past. "If I am making an argument identical to one made by David Hume, why is it not good enough to stand when I make it?" He would slow, frustrate,

62. Ibid.
63. Ibid.
64. Ibid.
65. Ibid., 1–2.

> and refuse to understand the arguments of the philosophers of reputation as well as any student's in a seminar.[66]

While many students and colleagues might have been put off by O. K.'s approach, Hustwit admired it: "The single greatest impression he gave me when I spoke in his presence was that he was listening. By this I do not mean what one usually means by that, namely that one is understanding and affirming what another is saying. What I mean is that he was listening so closely to what one was saying that one had better start to listen to oneself."[67]

O. K. Bouwsma on Philosophy

Hustwit notes that O. K. was fond of saying that one *does* philosophy. By this he meant that philosophy does not constitute a body of knowledge. Contrasting himself with his son, he said to Hustwit: "Bill knows things. He knows a lot. I don't know anything."[68]

O. K. Bouwsma's Humor

Hustwit suggests that Bouwsma's use of humor was "an integral part of his work and character," and adds:

> I do not believe that he would use it against someone [whom] he did not think bright and able. He would use it against any serious philosophy student. He would use it to bring someone to self-examination. Everyone who met him or heard him read a paper or response or sat in on a seminar has a humorous anecdote to relate. He did on-the-spot comedy; I never heard him tell a joke. He was the master of every situation. He always had a quip, a pun, a chuckle which he sometimes covered in fake surprise, [and] it was not something that he could turn on and off. He certainly did not reserve it for philosophy alone.[69]

Impressive as it may have been, not everyone appreciated his humor. Beverly Bouwsma noted that:

66. Ibid., 3–4

67. Ibid., 4.

68. Ibid.

69. Ibid., 12.

> In their later years Gertrude and [O. K.] would come out here every summer and would stay in a house across the street from us and have dinner with us very often so there was a lot of conversation. [O. K.] would "tease," as I am sure he thought of it as, Bill and the boys . . . but never our daughter or me. And when it got too bad I would always give him a look and he would quit.[70]

She continued:

> Our poor sons would talk in an ordinary way about their lives and he would pick out an inappropriate word or one he thought had a doubtful meaning and [would give] them a hard time about it. "What do you mean about that?" would be a usual way he would put it and the poor boys would go sort of crazy trying to explain what they meant. Bill would resent this kind of criticism and so would I and certainly so would they. Gertrude would look baffled but so used to it that it didn't seem at all odd to her.[71]

It does not seem too far-fetched to suggest that such "teasing" and constant interrogation would create in Bouwsma a deep sense of anxiety about the meaning of his words.[72]

Going to Church with the Bouwsmas

Early in their relationship, O. K. asked Hustwit if he would drive him and his wife to church on Sunday mornings. Though there were plenty of churches in Lincoln, O. K. wanted to go to Omaha for church, which meant driving 120 miles (roundtrip) each Sunday. Hustwit agreed. Hustwit notes that the "Bouwsmas attended the Christian Reformed Church which is a splinter of the Dutch Reformed Church," and adds, "I do not understand the division to this day, though I understood the former to be more conservative and evangelical than the latter. Whatever the differences, one knew in one visit that John Calvin had been there."[73] O. K. told Hustwit that he came to love

70. Personal Communication, October 20, 2008.

71. Personal Communication, October 20, 2008. See, too, Lage, "Beverly Bouwsma," 45.

72. Also see Lage, "Bouwsma," 41.

73. Hustwit, *Something about O. K. Bouwsma*, 14. For more on Dutch Calvinism, see Bratt, *Dutch Calvinism*. As a boy, O. K. did not allow Bouwsma to have lunch with his friends on Sundays because he believed that this would have violated the Sabbath. See Lage, "Bouwsma," 8.

a certain expression of Christianity and that one "gets used to that expression and then everything else seems foreign by comparison to it" and that "it should not be changed."[74]

One may wonder why O. K., a staunch Calvinist, was interested in the philosophy of Wittgenstein. Hustwit asked O. K. this very question during their first trip to Omaha, and he replied by talking about Wittgenstein's notion of theology as grammar: "If one pays attention to grammar—to how a word gets used in everyday expressions and surroundings—then one will know what to do with it when it confuses him in philosophy. It is a kind of a map or a key which tells one how to proceed."[75] Further, "[t]he Scriptures are a kind of map or key which tell one how to proceed. Theology is not inventing what to say about God . . . . [Theologians] must retell what is already there."[76] For O. K., Christianity was not a philosophical system but rather a way of life: "If all problems of philosophy were merely problems of language, if all philosophical problems could be 'dissolved,' what was left?"[77] Nothing. But Christianity, O. K. reasoned, cannot be dissolved *because* it is not a philosophical system.

O. K. Bouwsma's Father

Hustwit noted that O. K.'s death affected him like the death of a father. After a memorial service for O. K., Hustwit had the opportunity to talk with Angelyn Stevens, O. K.'s sister, and she told him a story about O. K. and his father. During summers while he was still completing his graduate studies, he would work at the golf course his father owned. In exchange for the work, O. K. and his wife were given room and board. Hustwit then recounts this scene:

> At dinner one night the talk turned to Darwin and evolution. [O. K.] was explaining and defending Darwin's theory to the consternation of his father. Their father finally had enough of it, and pronounced that he would not eat with someone who believed him descended from a monkey . . . . [O. K.] and Gertrude [then] had to take their meals to the cabin to eat.[78]

74. Hustwit, *Something about O. K. Bouwsma*, 15.

75. Ibid., 16.

76. Ibid. On this point, see Craig Barnes, *The Pastor as Minor Poet*.

77. Hustwit, *Something about O. K. Bouwsma*, 22.

78. Ibid., 31.

It seems plausible that O. K.'s commitment to "doing" rather than "knowing" might have been another reason that Wittgenstein became important for O. K. because now he would never have to defend Darwin—or any other body of knowledge—and could focus instead on the relationships of words. If, according to O. K., there was no progress in philosophy—that is, no evolution—this was also personally true for O. K. in that the question that O. K. struggled with, both at the beginning of his professional life and at the end, was, *what is the meaning of a word?*

Individuation: Preliminary Steps

My basic argument in this chapter is, as noted, that Bouwsma individuated from his father and his father's religion by means of his scholarship, specifically by writing about Calvin. Bouwsma's previous scholarship helped, but the book on Calvin was key because Calvin was the central theological thinker in his father's religion. In this section, I demonstrate how Bouwsma used the study of Calvin to individuate from his father. Before doing so, however, I show how Bouwsma used previous scholarship in this regard as well.

Rome and Venice, Father and Son

In *Venice and the Defense of Republican Liberty*, published in 1968, Bouwsma states in the acknowledgements that he felt "some obligation to note here that the latter stages of my work were accomplished during the disorders that have agitated Berkeley since 1964, and these well-publicized events have taught me a good deal about the realities that underlie political discourse."[79] (The events to which Bouwsma is referring involve the civil unrest in Berkeley relating to civil rights, free speech, and the Vietnam War.) He continues: "They have required of me, as of other academic men, some direct participation in the *vita activa civile*; and they considerably deepened my understanding of the relationship between political liberty and intellectual vitality, of the contradictions between idealism and political accommodation."[80] Bouwsma also notes that the events in Berkeley helped him to see "the tension between freedom and order and the terrible anxiet-

79. Bouwsma, *Venice and the Defense of Republican Liberty*, viii.

80. Ibid., vii.

ies this can generate in a crisis, and of the strain such anxieties impose on the sense of community."[81] Bouwsma points out that his original intention for the book was to write about Paolo Sarpi (1552–1623), a Venetian scholar and reformer, but as he progressed in his research the book became about the tension between Venice and the Counter Reformation (i.e., Rome).

My correspondence with Beverly Bouwsma proved especially useful for understanding Bouwsma's personal motivations for writing this book. She mentioned that Bouwsma was a "very hard worker" and a "troubled person."[82] When, in a subsequent letter, I asked her what she meant by "troubled," she replied: "I don't mean that he was crazy. He certainly wasn't," and continued:

> [H]e was very often depressed as I know because of living with him for sixty years and because sometimes he liked to talk to me about his problems. Quite often, in fact, and I was always interested in listening. This was particularly true when he was writing his Venice book, which he thought was about Rome (his father) against Venice (Bill) which maybe you have read. Well, anyway, that's the sort of troubled he was.[83]

Bouwsma's association of himself with Venice and his father with Rome is striking especially in light of the fact that Bouwsma was writing the book during the 1960s (which he described as a struggle between two generations concerning liberty and order). I suggest that this—i.e., making a case for Venice over Rome, one generation over another—is a concrete example of Bouwsma's individuation from his father. It is also worth noting that Bouwsma writes in the epilogue: "This book has been concerned with the contribution of the Venetians themselves to the formation and development of the powerful myth of Venice as *the ideal combination of liberty and order*."[84] This tension between liberty and order is, as we have seen in his book on Calvin, a tension that Bouwsma dealt with throughout his career.

81. Ibid.

82. Personal Correspondence, September 11, 2008.

83. Personal Correspondence, October 20, 2008. See, too, Lage, "Beverly Bouwsma," 42–44.

84. Bouwsma, *Venice and the Defense of Republican Liberty*, 628, emphasis mine. However, in an interview with Anne Lage, Bouwsma also noted that this was a tension that he observed in his father, but it manifested itself as a tension between Socratic inquiry (liberty) and Calvinist orthodoxy (order). See Lage, "Bouwsma," 4.

On the Origins of the Humanities

By siding with Venice over Rome, Bouwsma took a step down the path of individuation. He took more steps down this path by locating the origins of the humanities in Protagoras (a Sophist) over Socrates (Plato's mentor). In "Socrates and the Confusion of the Humanities," a chapter originally published in 1982 but begun during the 1976–1977 academic year when Bouwsma was a member in the National Humanities Institute, Bouwsma traces the beginnings of the humanities and looks at the role of Socrates in particular.[85] He argues that the humanities have their root in antiquity, particularly in the split within philosophy between a search for ultimate truth on the one hand and, on the other hand, rhetoric. The basic confusion in the humanities, as Bouwsma sees it, is whether the goal is to obtain ultimate truth or if the truth of the situation is that humankind is the measure of all things. Is the task of the humanities, in other words, certitude about the world and human nature, or is the task to reflect upon the human condition, deeply, rigorously, and honestly, knowing full well that all knowledge is contingent and limited? Bouwsma suggests the latter and argues that "[r]hetoric, not philosophy, gave us the humanities"[86] and that the humanities begin with Protagoras and not Socrates. Locating the humanities in rhetoric (and not philosophy) and in Protagoras (and not Socrates) seems to have been, at least in part, a critique of O. K., who considered himself a modern day Socrates; this was not unlike siding with Venice over Rome.

Individuation and the Creation of Meaning: A "Usable" Calvin

If by siding with Venice over Rome Bouwsma took a step down the path of individuation, and if he took more such steps by locating the origins of the humanities in Protagoras over Socrates, I suggest that he successfully individuated from his father by writing about Calvin. In what follows I draw on selected features of Bouwsma's portrait of Calvin that provide evidence for this claim.

85. Bouwsma, "Socrates and the Confusion of the Humanities."

86. Ibid., 388.

A Family Book

The subtext of *John Calvin* is about family—*Bouwsma's family*. Given their Dutch Calvinist heritage, the dedication of the book to his wife and children is telling in this regard: "To Beverly and to John, Philip, Paul, and Sarah for a better understanding of ourselves."[87] In the opening pages of the book, Bouwsma notes the "very human tendency to invent the fathers we need," and suggests that the statue of Calvin in Geneva at the Reformers' Wall is an example of this need: "Unlike the human Calvin, the statue is difficult to forget, as of course it was intended to be; it is, after all, a memorial. But it is a good deal more than that."[88] He continues:

> For here Calvin stands, more than twice as large as life, stylized beyond recognition, stony, rigid, immobile, and—except for his slightly abstracted disapproval of whatever we might imagine him to be contemplating—impassive. Drained of humanity, this *man*, who was singularly eloquent about the universality of human frailty and who, in his own life, was constantly looking within himself for reminders that no human being is ever free from the struggle with sin and weakness, has been converted into an icon in order to create an impression and to stimulate a degree of veneration about which his own views might be interesting to hear.[89]

A major purpose of Bouwsma's book, then, is to demonstrate that the Calvin as given by later Calvinism is an invention and, we might assume, an invented father that we might live *without*. Also, Bouwsma is giving his family a Calvin—a father—that they might be able to live *with*.

Liberty and Order

As noted, a central feature of Bouwsma's portrait of Calvin is that Calvin struggled with a tension in himself between liberty and order. This tension led Bouwsma to suggest that there were two Calvins. One Calvin was philosophical and rational and craved order and certainty; this Calvin distrusted freedom and the world and sought to control the forces both in himself and in the world. The other Calvin was rhetorical and humanistic. This Calvin celebrated paradoxes and mysteries and valued experience over theory; he

87. Bouwsma, *John Calvin*, ix.

88. Ibid., 1–2.

89. Ibid., 2.

was generally more flexible and tolerant than the other Calvin. I also noted above that Bouwsma was more interested in the tensions rather than the harmonies in western culture (which he attributed to the fact that he was the son of "second-generation Dutch Calvinist immigrants who were trying to assimilate the high culture of early-twentieth-century America"[90]) and that he noted that these tensions posed problems for him. One problem involved "the compatibility of an 'inalienable right' to 'life, liberty, and the pursuit of happiness' [i.e., liberty] with Christianity [i.e., order]."[91] By writing about these two Calvins—by demonstrating a tension within Calvin that involved liberty and order—Bouwsma was able to address the (in)compatibility of liberty and order within himself. If, in previous work, Bouwsma made a case for liberty (Venice) over order (Rome), here he was able to advocate both liberty and order in the form of a composite. I suggest that the latter indicates a successful individuation in that Bouwsma's differentiation was less defensive—the son did not need to defeat the father—as it was enough to coexist in the form of a composite.

Anxiety

Anxiety was a personal, not simply an academic, issue for Bouwsma. In his book on Calvin, Bouwsma does not come out and simply say, "I am an anxious person," but, what is striking about his analysis of Calvin, neither did Calvin. Indeed, Bouwsma notes that Calvin "disclosed himself . . . in broad, protective generalities whose truth is less than obvious."[92] Bouwsma notes, "Every Christian, or every human being, [Calvin] may assert, has had such and such experience, is convinced of this or that. But if we ask how he can know this, the answer may often be that he was thinking of himself."[93] If we accept Bouwsma's method in assessing statements of Calvin, is this not also an invitation to read similar statements made by Bouwsma in the same way? I think so. Here is one such statement from Bouwsma: "All human beings may be anxious; some, individually, in groups, and from time to time, are more anxious than others."[94] I suggest that we can turn Bouwsma's method back on himself and ask the same question that he asked of Calvin:

90. Bouwsma, "Introduction," 8.

91. Ibid.

92. Bouwsma, *John Calvin*, 5.

93. Ibid.

94. Ibid., 32.

"But if we ask how he can know this, the answer may often be that he was thinking of himself."[95] In writing about Calvin's anxiety, he was writing about his own.

Bouwsma notes that Calvin saw anxiety everywhere: "in episodes recorded in Scripture, the study of which occupied so much of his mature life, and among his contemporaries."[96] Bouwsma, too, saw anxiety everywhere. Bouwsma writes that his "interest in the relation between anxiety and culture was first stimulated by [Johan] Huizinga's *Waning of the Middle Ages*."[97] In a footnote, he adds that this relationship, though implied in his essays "Three Types of Historiography in Post-Renaissance Italy" (published in 1965) and "Christian Adulthood" (published in 1976), did not become "prominent" until his "Anxiety and the Formation of Early Modern Culture" (published in 1980).[98] Yet his full-treatment of anxiety did not come about until his book on Calvin. Bouwsma's book on Calvin was published in 1988, but he published an article on Calvin's anxiety in *The Proceedings of the American Philosophical Society* in 1984, meaning that he was working on it in the mid-1980s when he was in his sixties and nearing retirement, during the decade after the death of his father. Coming to terms with anxiety, individuation, and the death of his father seem to be intertwined in Bouwsma's life and work.

Lack of Progress

Another feature of Bouwsma's book on Calvin is that he calls it a *portrait*. He invokes the word portrait for a specific reason because he conceives of portraits as static. His reconstruction is of a man, Calvin, who was static in that he progressed very little in the personal and intellectual issues that he was dealing with over the course of his life; this aspect of Bouwsma's portrait of Calvin has resonances with Bouwsma's father, who, as Hustwit pointed out, was struggling with the same questions at the end of his career than at the beginning ("What is the meaning of a word?"). Thus, it can hardly be insignificant that Bouwsma creates a portrait of Calvin who made very little progress in his personal and intellectual life.

95. Ibid., 5.

96. Ibid., 37.

97. Bouwsma, "Introduction," 11.

98. Ibid., 16, see note 34.

On Knowing Things

I also noted above that O. K. would make statements such as "Bill knows things," "He knows a lot," and "I don't know anything," but that these statements were not meant in praise, precisely because O. K. did not believe in progress in philosophy. I suggest that Bouwsma returned the favor by portraying Calvin as a man who had made no progress, and that this, too, was not meant as praise.[99] Yet Bouwsma was able to endorse a Calvin who recognized that the Bible could err (recall that Calvin argued that the Gospel of Matthew was incorrect about the star guiding the magi), whereas O. K. embraced Wittgenstein so as to embrace a pure, true, flawless, and ahistorical Calvinism.

CONCLUSION: RECOVERING RELIGION

As noted in the conclusions of the previous chapters, in this book I am interested in what I am broadly calling reversals and restorations of religion. Each of my subjects reverse and restore religion in their own way and in doing so use their own language. I suggest that the language that seems most appropriate for Bouwsma in this regard is recovering religion. The basis for this suggestion is that the loss for Bouwsma in terms of religion involved his rejection of his father's Dutch Calvinism by means of recovering, with the tools of history, a humane and humanistic Calvin. I am not suggesting, though, that Bouwsma once accepted Dutch Calvinism and then came to reject it; he was probably never quite comfortable with it. Indeed, when I asked Beverly Bouwsma about his faith and beliefs, she was uncertain as to whether or not to call him a Christian:

> But was he a Christian? I think he was most of the time, although I think not fully and often he wouldn't go to church for long periods. I took his course called History of Christianity, which was entirely historical and I believe that it would have been the same whether he was or was not a Christian.[100]

99. Indeed, Bouwsma noted in an interview that his father neither respected nor read his work. See Lage, "Bouwsma," 15.

100. Personal Correspondence, September 11, 2008. Also, Bouwsma himself noted that his faith is something that, at times, is strong but, at other times, is virtually absent, and that his faith is filled with skepticism. Also see Lage, "Bouwsma," 120. Beverley Bouwsma recalls that her first year of marriage with Bouwsma was filled with fighting, and that most of the fights involved religion. See Lage, "Beverly Bouwsma," 12.

So it is not quite right to suggest that he once embraced Dutch Calvinism, lost it, and then found new religious meaning; the mourning religion thesis needs to be understood and applied differently than this in the case of Bouwsma.

In the case of Bouwsma, all three stages of the mourning religion thesis, similarly to the case of Dittes, to some extent occurred at once in a mixed way while he was writing his book on Calvin. Bouwsma, who never had the relationship with his father that he craved[101] (stage one of Homans's theory), individuated from his father's Dutch Calvinism[102] by writing his book on Calvin (stage two of Homans's theory), scholarship that Bouwsma undertook during the 1980s[103] after the death of his father in 1978. Bouwsma then forged his own spirituality by recovering a historical Calvin that was useable for him (stage three of Homans's theory). It is worth noting that Bouwsma seemed to identify with Calvin in some way in that, just as a humanist education gave Calvin the tools to challenge his own tradition by providing "an opening" out of his traditional culture (Roman Catholicism), a humanities education gave Bouwsma the tools to find "an opening" out of his traditional culture (Dutch Calvinism). Bouwsma could not or would not simply reject Calvin; he had to, it seems, recover Calvin from his father for himself and for his own family.[104]

It is also worth noting that Bouwsma quotes William James to intimate his own view of humanistic scholarship: "What the system claims to be . . . is a picture of the great universe of God. What it is—and oh so flagrantly—is the revelation of how intensely odd the personal flavor of some fellow creature is."[105] Elaborating on this point, Bouwsma writes, "I believe that one of the basic tasks of humanistic scholarship is to discover the personal, and therefore historical, flavor that constitutes the humanity of all cultural artifacts."[106] The goal, then, of his book on Calvin is to discover the personal and historical flavor of Calvin as a human being—a goal that

101. In an interview with Lage, Bouwsma noted that he was born on his father's birthday, and he felt sure that he was a birthday gift that his father did not want to receive. See Lage, "Bouwsma," 12.

102. Strikingly, Bouwsma notes that, years after writing his book on Calvin, he came to see that he was seeking his independence from his father by writing it. Also see Lage, "Bouwsma," 105.

103. See Bouwsma, *Calvin*, vi.

104. Ibid., ix. Also see Lage, "Bouwsma," 34, 38.

105. Bouwsma, *Calvin*, 3.

106. Ibid.

has been neglected by the two primary groups that have studied Calvin: specialists (who have focused on what Calvin read) and faith communities (who have studied what Calvin wrote). Bouwsma does so by, as noted, positing two Calvins—the traditional rigid and philosophical Calvin, and the neglected humanistic and rhetorical Calvin. Both of these Calvins existed in the historical Calvin, not as a synthesis but as a composite. Bouwsma notes that his portrait will not please any particular group of Calvinists. Regarding the division between scholars and religious believers, however, Bouwsma believes that his portrait will be one that is not easily dismissed by either group because his Calvin is one that is dogmatic but not as dogmatic as religious believers have presented him to be. In doing so Bouwsma reversed the tendency of making Calvin larger-than-life by restoring Calvin's humanity.

Bouwsma's portrait is itself a personal, and therefore historical, artifact. By emphasizing certain features of Calvin's life—namely, that Calvin never spoke warmly about his father; that Calvin's Geneva represented a reproach of the past (and, therefore, his own father); that Calvin was a reclusive intellectual who was driven into the active life; and that Calvin was a humanist—Bouwsma identified with Calvin in that Bouwsma never spoke warmly about his father; Bouwsma's portrait of Calvin represented a kind of reproach of past religious and secular interpretations of Calvin (especially those of his father's Dutch Calvinism); Bouwsma was a reclusive intellectual who as an administrator at Berkeley during the 1960s was driven into the active life; and Bouwsma was a humanist. In *John Calvin*, Bouwsma's chief accomplishment was the restoration of a rhetorical reformer, a Calvin who was "particularly sensitive to the subtleties and contradictions of the human condition."[107] This sensitive Calvin made Bouwsma less anxious. Perhaps *this* Calvin will do the same for others.

107. Ibid., 234.

Conclusion

> Many readers as well as myself have experienced grief at the monstrous volume of anti-Christianity discoverable in the history of Christianity. The history of Christianity, which ought to unite men in competing for the realization of love of Jesus in every walk of life, in fact revealed innumerable instances of savage and uncharitable disputes about dogmas, sacraments, and ecclesiastical powers.
>
> —Oskar Pfister[1]

THOU ART THE MAN

In the Bible (2 Samuel), Nathan was a prophet to David, who is often held up as the greatest king of Israel. His interaction with Nathan, however, does not concern greatness but moral failure. One spring day when David rose in the afternoon and happened to be walking on his roof, he saw a beautiful woman bathing on another roof. David sent one of his servants to inquire about this woman, and it was reported to him that her name was Bathsheba and that she was married to Uriah, one of David's best and most loyal warriors. At the time, Uriah was away fighting for David. So David sent for Bathsheba. They slept together, and she became pregnant.

Later, Bathsheba sent a message to David informing him that she was pregnant. He puzzled over what to do. He decided to recall Uriah from the battlefield. They talked about how the war was going, and at the close of their conversation David instructed Uriah to go down to his house, hoping that Uriah would sleep with Bathsheba (so that the pregnancy could be attributed to Uriah). Uriah, however, slept outside of his house and refused

1. Pfister, *Christianity and Fear*, 9.

to be intimate with his wife. The following day David received word of this and then asked Uriah why he did not sleep in his house with Bathsheba. Uriah replied that he would not do such a thing while they were at war; David's plan failed.

The following day David tried again. This time Uriah and David ate and drank alcohol together, but Uriah still would not sleep with his wife. David, as expected, was very dissatisfied with this turn of events. It was now clear that he would have to take responsibility for Bathsheba's pregnancy. But instead of taking responsibility, David devised an even more sinister plan than his previous one. When Uriah went back to the battlefield, David sent word to one of his commanding officers to put Uriah in the front lines and to draw back so that Uriah would be killed. The officer put Uriah in the most difficult fighting position, and he was killed. When Bathsheba heard this, she grieved deeply. When she had finished mourning, David brought her into his house, and she bore him a son.

David's actions greatly displeased the LORD. And so the LORD sent Nathan to David. Nathan told the following parable to David, which was presented to David as an actual occurrence:

> There were two men in one city; the one rich, and the other poor. The rich man had exceeding many flocks and herds: But the poor man had nothing, save one little ewe lamb, which he had bought and nourished up: and it grew up together with him, and with his children; it did eat of his own meat, and drank of his own cup, and lay in his bosom, and was unto him as a daughter. And there came a traveler unto the rich man, and he spared to take of his own flock and of his own herd, to dress for the wayfaring man that was come unto him; but took the poor man's lamb, and dressed it for the man that was come to him. (2 Samuel 12.1–4, KJV)

The narrative continues: "And David's anger was greatly kindled against the man; and he said to Nathan, As the LORD liveth, the man that hath done this thing shall surely die: And he shall restore the lamb fourfold, because he did this thing, and because he had no pity. And Nathan said to David, Thou art the man" (2 Samuel 12.5–7a, KJV). Nathan, cleverly, had shown David his own sin.

A central meaning of the parable seems to be that David acted like the rich man, taking Bathsheba (i.e., Uriah's only "sheep") from Uriah, who stood for the poor man. David had many wives—i.e., many "sheep"—so there was no need for him to take another man's only sheep/wife. On this reading, the parable is obviously sexist and androcentric, viewing women as sexual property.[2] Another problem with this reading is that Uriah was the one who was killed, not Bathsheba. So perhaps the story could be read with Bathsheba as the poor man who had her only sheep taken away from her and killed. In any case, on either reading the parable is prophetic in that David is in the wrong.

PLAYING NATHAN

I have always identified with the prophet Nathan in the Bible, believing that it was (and is) my calling to be a prophet like him. When I was a teenager, I believed that this meant that I was called to be a pastor—as pastors, like prophets, are the ones who claim to be speaking for God, just as Nathan spoke for God—but as a teenager I neglected the prophetic aspect of Nathan's office. Today I am even more inclined to aspire to be like Nathan because Nathan was not afraid to confront the highest of authorities when they were in the wrong; I hope one day to have his courage and integrity.

I have been attracted to psychology of religion and pastoral theology because I see these disciplines as prophetic. To me it is as though pastoral theologians and psychologists of religion say "thou art the man" (Nathan's rebuke of David) to the dominant voices and authorities in Christian traditions. In this book, I have focused on the prophetic stands of Capps, Dittes, and Bouwsma—how they have played Nathan, how they, that is to say, have used their scholarship to reverse and to restore religion.

A SUMMARY OF MY ARGUMENT

To recap, in this book I have examined reversals and restorations apparent in psychological portraits of three of the most influential figures in church history—Jesus, Augustine, and Calvin. These portraits have emphasized the reverse of what one usually finds in strands of traditional Christianity: Capps focused on what Jesus did (not what was done to him); Dittes focused on Augustine's method of introspection (i.e., his way of asking questions) rather than his solutions; and Bouwsma focused on Calvin's humanity (not his "saintliness"). All three of these prophetic reversals also turn out to be faithful restorations. That is, these portraits are all endorsements of religion

2. On this point, see Countryman, *Dirt, Greed, and Sex*.

in and for contemporary life: for Capps, Jesus provides a model for how men might address their own melancholia; for Dittes, Augustine teaches us the religious value of restlessness; and for Bouwsma, understanding Calvin's anxieties can help us reduce our own.

Pointing out this dynamic of reversals and restorations in what might be called the psychohistory of Christianity is an important observation in its own right. But my project does not stop there in that I explain this dynamic, in part, in terms of the mourning religion thesis. In the case of Capps, I argue that Capps addressed various losses in a deeply personal way during his fifties and that the key moment for Capps in overcoming his melancholia occurred after he applied his melancholia theory to Jesus. I argue this because there, in that text on Jesus, Capps was able to integrate and to sustain in a satisfying way his various selves and, therefore, open himself up to mourn in a non-defensive way—the way of humor. After Capps had written his book on Jesus, he was able subsequently to create a religious typology for men based on honor, hope, and humor.

While the various stages of the mourning religion thesis can be more or less observed sequentially in Capps's life, these stages do not fit so neatly in the case of Dittes. So I suggested that a variation of Homans's thesis—specifically, Cohler's notion of adaptive melancholia—more aptly described the relationship between Dittes's life and work. I argued that Dittes had a melancholic relationship with religion in that religion both created and alleviated his dissatisfaction with life, what Dittes described as his chronic sense of the shadows of destiny. I suggested, moreover, that this melancholic relationship was rooted in the fact that he was born the day after Christmas to a mother named Mary and a father who was a carpenter. It seems to me that this boy was sure to grow up with a sense of destiny and that it was inevitable that this Mary had messianic hopes for her son—this, it also seems to me, would likely make any son restless. In writing about Augustine and Augustine's relationship with his mother, Dittes was able to mourn and to recall his own personal sense of destiny by focusing on Augustine's restlessness and later advocating the process of maturing into boyhood.

The mourning religion thesis again looks different when applied to Bouwsma, where all three stages of the mourning religion thesis appear to be happening at once. If it is clear in the case of Dittes that Dittes did, finally, hold onto his religion, it is not so clear in the case of Bouwsma. Since Bouwsma's father's own identity was so tied up in Dutch Calvinism, individuating from Dutch Calvinism and his father was a difficult (and anxiety provoking) process, and it took writing a book on Calvin's anxiety to do such personal work. I argued that, just as a humanist education gave Calvin the tools to challenge his own tradition by providing a way out of his traditional culture (Roman Catholicism), a humanities education gave Bouwsma the tools to find a way out of his traditional culture (Dutch Calvinism). Yet, I also argued, Bouwsma could not or would not simply reject Calvin because he had to recover Calvin from his father for himself. The Calvin that Bouwsma found personally useful was a rhetorical Calvin—work that Bouwsma began after the death of his father.

THE LIMITS OF THE MOURNING RELIGION THESIS

While I believe the mourning religion thesis is extremely helpful in thinking about the relationship between a scholar's life and work (especially scholars who work in some version of religion and psychology), there are limitations to the thesis. The relationship between a scholar's life and work is not only one of mourning. Once when I was talking informally with a biblical scholar about this thesis and how it might apply to her life, she didn't think that it did and suggested instead that a better way of understanding the relationship between her life and work was liberation because she was able to break away from the constraining orthodoxy of her youth. Another way of putting this is as follows: Do religious feminists need to mourn patriarchal religion? Maybe there is nothing there for them to mourn.[3]

There are also persons and groups in religious studies who are not mourning religion at all because they are "caretakers" of religion.[4] Some scholars in the Society for Biblical Literature, for example, have the reputation of being rigorous in their methodology in terms of historical-criticism and language analysis but also have the reputation of being apologists for Christianity. Professors at theological seminaries and divinity schools, too, often write from an explicitly confessional point of view.[5] Thus, sometimes religion has not been lost at all.

Additionally, the focus on mourning might be overly negative. Just as Freud is sometimes criticized for constructing a psychology of "the

3. See Brock and Parker, *Proverbs of Ashes.*

4. McCutcheon, *Critics not Caretakers.*

5. See, e.g., Allen, *Christian Belief in a Postmodern World.*

basement" (as opposed to transpersonal psychology's psychology of "the attic"[6]), the mourning religion thesis might be criticized for excluding factors such as curiosity and joy as primary links between a scholar's life and work.

Finally, the relationship between a scholar's life and work might be thought of in terms of sublimation. Can we not imagine cases where religious studies scholars sublimate their own sexuality into their work? All of this is to say, quite simply, that there are a number of ways in which we can think about what religious studies scholars are doing in their work, and mourning is a helpful category in this regard but is by no means the only category.

A BENEDICTION: PASTORAL SCAVENGERS AS REVERSERS AND RESTORERS OF RELIGION

Robert Dykstra notes that Valerie DeMarinis, a pastoral theologian, once heard two of her colleagues, who both were systematic theologians, talk about the field of pastoral theology. She writes:

> The topic was pastoral psychology in general, and the pastoral practitioner in particular. One said to the other, "They are just like scavengers. They have no real theory, just a hunting and pecking, a grabbing and applying. There is no order for them. And they can never explain what they do or why they do it, only that something works or not. It is all technique, and at best has some rationale to measure if it works. It is a very sad state of affairs.[7]

Dykstra adds, "DeMarinis acknowledges that while she was initially troubled by the disparaging nature of this professor's depiction of her field, on further reflection she came to embrace the image."[8] That is, she reversed this criticism and turned it into a virtue of her discipline by recognizing that scavengers are actually "highly skilled at collecting, extracting, and cleansing" and that the "responsible scavenger is one skilled at survival,

6. See Maslow, *Religions, Values, and Peak-Experiences*; Goble, *The Third Force*; Ferrer, *Revisioning Transpersonal Theory*. Also see Carlin and Capps, *100 Years of Happiness*, 73–74; and Seligman, *Flourish*.

7. Quoted in Dykstra, *Images of Pastoral Care*, 9.

8. Ibid.

one who knows how to search, salvage, purify, and transform the elements of the world into that which nurtures and sustains life."[9]

Psychologists of religion and pastoral theologians may indeed be scavengers, but scavengers are a part of God's good creation. God calls these scavengers to pick through what has been thrown away. Following this call, Capps, Dittes, and Bouwsma have scavenged through the lives of Jesus, Augustine, and Calvin to reframe, to recall, and to recover—in other words, to reverse and to restore—religion that is rich with experience, including (and especially) their own.[10] It seems to me that this restorative work, this scavenging, inevitably involves introspection that leads, in part, to mourning, and that this mourning of and with religion is itself a religious act: It is *religious* mourning. So following Capps, Dittes, and Bouwsma—as well as Pfister, DeMarinis, and Dykstra—may we all reverse and restore religion such that it is rich with experience and in so doing work as scavengers for the realization of the love of Jesus Christ in every walk of life, mourning if need be.

9. Ibid.

10. Cf. Dittes, "The Investigator as an Instrument of Investigation"; Capps, "Shame, Melancholy, and the Introspective Method."

Bibliography

Allen, Diogenes. *Christian Belief in a Postmodern World: The Full Wealth of Conviction*. Louisville, KY: Westminster John Knox Press, 1989.

Ariès, Philippe. *The Hour of Our Death: The Classic History of Western Attitudes toward Death over the Last One Thousand Years*. Translated by Helen Weaver. New York: Vintage Books, 2008.

Augustine. *The Confessions of St. Augustine*. Translated by Rex Warner. New York: Mentor, 1963.

Bakan, David. *Sigmund Freud and the Jewish Mystical Tradition*. Mineola, NY: Dover Publications, Inc., 2004.

Barnes, M. Craig. *The Pastor as Minor Poet: Pastoral Calling and Identity in the Twenty-First Century*. Grand Rapids, MI: William B. Eerdmans, 2009.

Belzen, Jacob. "Mourning Religion? Celebrating Transformation! From Loss to Gain, from Depression to Melancholia." *Pastoral Psychology* 59 (2010) 347–353.

———, editor. *Psychology of Religion: Autobiographical Accounts*. New York: Springer, 2012.

Bingaman, Kirk. *Freud and Faith: Living in the Tension*. New York: SUNY, 2003.

Birch, Bruce, Walter Brueggemann, Terence Fretheim, and David Petersen. *A Theological Introduction to the Old Testament*. Nashville, TN: Abingdon Press, 1999.

Bouwsma, William. "Christian Adulthood." In *A Useable Past: Essays in European Cultural History*, edited by William Bouwsma, 397–417. Berkeley, CA: University of California Press, 1990.

———. "Introduction." In *A Useable Past: Essays in European Cultural History*, edited by William Bouwsma, 1–16. Berkeley, CA: University of California Press, 1990.

———. *John Calvin: A Sixteenth Century Portrait*. New York and Oxford: Oxford University Press, 1988.

———. "Socrates and the Confusion of the Humanities." In *A Useable Past: Essays in European Cultural History*, edited by William Bouwsma, 385–396. Berkeley, CA: University of California Press, 1990.

———. *Venice and the Defense of Republican Liberty: Renaissance Values in the Age of the Counter Reformation*. Berkeley, CA: University of California Press, 1968.

Boym, Svetlana. *The Future of Nostalgia*. New York: Basic Books, 2001.

Bratt, James. *Dutch Calvinism in Modern America: A History of a Conservative Subculture*. Eugene, OR: Wipf and Stock Publishers, 2002.

Brock, Rita, and Rebecca Parker. *Proverbs of Ashes: Violence, Redemptive Suffering, and the Search for What Saves Us*. Boston: Beacon Press, 2001.

Brucker, Gene. "In Memoriam: William J. Bouwsma." *Perspectives on History: The Newsmagazine of the American Historical Association*. September, 2004. On-line: http://www.historians.org/publications-and-directories/perspectives-on-history/september-2004/in-memoriam-william-j-bouwsma.

Capps, Donald. *Agents of Hope: A Pastoral Psychology*. Eugene, OR: Wipf and Stock, 2001.

———. *At Home in the World: A Study in Psychoanalysis, Religion, and Art*. Eugene, OR: Cascade Books, 2013.

———. *The Child's Song: The Religious Abuse of Children*. Louisville, KY: Westminster John Knox Press, 1995.

———. *The Decades of Life: A Guide to Human Development*. Louisville, KY: Westminster John Knox Press, 2008.

———. "Forty Years with Moses." *Pastoral Psychology* 58 (2009) 451–462.

———. *Fragile Connections: Memoirs of Mental Illness for Pastoral Care Professionals*. St. Louis, MO: Chalice Press, 2005.

———. *Giving Counsel: A Minister's Guidebook*. St. Louis, MO: Chalice Press, 2001.

———. "James E. Dittes: A Professional Portrait." *Pastoral Psychology* 52 (2003) 17–49.

———. *Jesus: A Psychological Biography*. St. Louis, MO: Chalice Press, 2000.

———. *Jesus the Village Psychiatrist*. Louisville, KY: Westminster John Knox Press, 2008.

———. *Laughter Ever After: Ministry of Good Humor*. St. Louis, MO: Chalice, 2008.

———. "The Letting Loose of Hope: Where Psychology of Religion and Pastoral Care Converge." *Journal of Pastoral Care* 51 (1997) 139–149.

———. *Life Cycle Theory and Pastoral Care*. Eugene, OR: Wipf and Stock, 2002.

———. *Living Stories: Pastoral Counseling in Congregational Context*. Minneapolis, MN: Fortress Press, 1998.

———. *Men and Their Religion: Honor, Hope, and Humor*. Harrisburg, PA: Trinity Press International, 2002.

———. *Men, Religion, and Melancholia: James, Otto, Jung, and Erikson*. New Haven, CT: Yale University Press, 1997.

———. *Pastoral Care and Preaching: A Quest for an Integrated Ministry*. Philadelphia: The Westminster Press, 1980.

———. *Pastoral Care: A Thematic Approach*. Philadelphia: The Westminster Press, 1979.

———. *The Poet's Gift: Toward the Renewal of Pastoral Care*. Louisville, KY: Westminster/John Knox Press, 1993.

———. "Prejudice, Prodigality, and the Precariousness of Life." *Pastoral Psychology* 52 (2003) 123–145.

———. "The Psychological Benefits of Humor." *Pastoral Psychology* 54 (2006) 393–411.

———. *Reframing: A New Method in Pastoral Care*. Minneapolis, MN: Fortress Press, 1990.

———. "Shame, Melancholy, and the Introspective Method in Psychology of Religion." In *Taking a Step Back: Assessments of the Psychology of Religion*, edited by Jacob Belzen and Owe Wikström, 37–54. Uppsala: Acta Universitatis Upsaliensis, 1997.

———. "A Summary of Jesus." *Pastoral Psychology* 50 (2002) 391–400.

———. *A Time to Laugh: The Religion of Humor*. New York: Continuum, 2005.

———. *Young Clergy: A Biographical-Developmental Study*. New York: The Haworth Press, 2005.

Capps, John, and Donald Capps. *You've Got to Be Kidding: How Jokes Can Help You Think*. Chichester, West Sussex: Wiley-Blackwell, 2009.

Capps, Donald, and Nathan Carlin. "The Homosexual Tendencies of King James: Should this Matter to Bible Readers Today?" *Pastoral Psychology* 55 (2007) 667–699.

———. *Living in Limbo: Life in the Midst of Uncertainty.* Eugene, OR: Cascade Books, 2010.

Capps, Donald, and James Dittes, editors. *The Hunger of the Heart: Reflections on the* Confessions *of Augustine.* West Lafayette, IN: Society for the Scientific Study of Religion, 1990.

———. "Preface." In *The Hunger of the Heart: Reflections on the* Confessions *of Augustine*, edited by Donald Capps and James Dittes, vii-x. West Lafayette, IN: Society for the Scientific Study of Religion, 1990.

Capps, Donald, and Robert Dykstra. "Books and Articles by James E. Dittes." *Pastoral Psychology* 52 (2003) 185–189.

Capps, Walter. *Religious Studies: The Making of a Discipline.* Minneapolis, MN: Fortress Press, 1995.

Carlin, Nathan. "Dittes, James." In *Encyclopedia of Psychology and Religion*, edited by David Leeming, Kathryn Madden, and Stanton Marlan, 511–514. New York: Springer, 2014.

———. "Introduction to the Forum on Mourning Religion." *Pastoral Psychology* 59 (2010) 345.

———. "A Religious Experience: A Psychological Interpretation of Kevin Kelly's Conversion to Christianity." *Pastoral Psychology* 62 (2013) 587–605.

———. "Reversers and Restorers of Religion: Mourning and Meaning in Contemporary Psychological Portraits of Religious Leaders." PhD diss., Rice University, 2010.

———. "In Search of a More Reliable Truth: Mourning and Donald Capps's Psychological Portrait of Jesus." *Pastoral Psychology* 58 (2009) 463–476.

Carlin, Nathan, and Donald Capps. *100 Years of Happiness: Insights and Findings from the Experts.* Santa Barbara, CA: Praeger, 2012.

Carlin, Nathan, and Heba Khan. "Mourning, Memorials, and Religion: A Psychoanalytic Perspective on the Park51 Controversy." *Religions* 2 (2011) 114–131.

Cohler, Bertram. "Nostalgia and the Disenchantment with Modernity: Memory Books as Adaptive Response to Shoah." In *Mourning Religion*, edited by William Parsons, Daine Jonte-Pace, and Susan Henking, 201–219. Charlottesville and London: University of Virginia Press, 2008.

Countryman, L. William. *Dirt, Greed, and Sex: Sexual Ethics in the New Testament and Their Implications for Today.* Philadelphia: Fortress Press, 1988.

Crossan, John Dominic. *Jesus: A Revolutionary Biography.* San Francisco: Harper, 1994.

Dittes, James. "Augustine: Search for a Fail-Safe God to Trust." In *The Hunger of the Heart; Reflections on* The Confessions *of Augustine*, edited by Donald Capps and James E. Dittes, 255–264. West Lafayette, IN: Society for the Scientific Study of Religion, 1990.

———. "Continuities between the Life and Thought of Augustine." In *The Hunger of the Heart: Reflections on* The Confessions *of Augustine*, edited by Donald Capps and James E. Dittes, 117–131. West Lafayette, IN: Society for the Scientific Study of Religion, 1990.

———. *Driven by Hope: Men and Meaning.* Louisville, KY: Westminster John Knox Press, 1996.

———. "The Investigator as an Instrument of Investigation: Some Exploratory Observations on the Compleat Researcher." In *Encounter with Erikson: Historical*

Interpretation and Religious Biography, edited by Donald Capps, Walter Capps, and M. Gerald Bradford, 347–373. Santa Barbara, CA: Scholars Press, 1977.

———. *The Male Predicament: On Being a Man Today*. San Francisco: Harper, 1985.

———. *Men at Work: Life beyond the Office*. 2nd ed. Louisville, KY: Westminster John Knox Press, 1996.

———. *Minister on the Spot*. Philadelphia: Pilgrim Press, 1970.

———. *Re-calling Ministry*. Edited by Donald Capps. St. Louis, MO: Chalice Press, 1999.

———. "Some Accidents, Coincidents, and Intents." *Pastoral Psychology* 52 (2003) 5–16.

———. "Teaching Freud's Teachings." In *Teaching Freud*, edited by Diane Jonte-Pace, 258- 270. Oxford: Oxford University Press, 2003.

———. *When Work Goes Sour*. Philadelphia: Westminster Press, 1987.

Dykstra, Robert. *Images of Pastoral Care: Classic Readings*. St. Louis, MO: Chalice Press, 2005.

———. "Maturing into Boyhood: James E. Dittes on Men and Meaning." *Pastoral Psychology* 52 (2003) 111–121.

Dykstra, Robert, and Allan Cole Jr. "Books and Articles by Donald Capps." *Pastoral Psychology* 58 (2009) 681–693.

Dykstra, Robert, Allan Cole Jr., and Donald Capps. *The Faith and Friendships of Teenage Boys*. Louisville, KY: Westminster John Knox Press, 2012.

———. *Losers, Loners, and Rebels: The Spiritual Struggles of Boys*. Louisville, KY: Westminster John Knox Press, 2007.

Elledge, Paul. "The Professor and the Saint." *Pastoral Psychology* 52 (2003) 173–183.

Erikson, Erik. *Childhood and Society*. 2nd ed. New York: Norton, 1963.

———. *Young Man Luther: A Study in Psychoanalysis and History*. New York: Norton, 1958.

Fenn, Richard. *Time Exposure: The Experience of Time in Secular Societies*. Oxford and New York: Oxford University Press, 2001.

Ferrer, Jorge. *Revisioning Transpersonal Theory: A Participatory Vision of Human Spirituality*. New York: SUNY, 2002.

Freud, Sigmund. *Civilization and Its Discontents*. In *The Standard Edition of the Complete Psychological Works of Sigmund Freud*, translated and edited by James Strachey, volume 21, 57–145. London: Vintage, 2001. First published 1930.

———. *The Future of an Illusion*. In *The Standard Edition of the Complete Psychological Works of Sigmund Freud*, translated and edited by James Strachey, volume 21, 1–56. London: Vintage, 2001. First published 1927.

———. *The Interpretation of Dreams*. In *The Standard Edition of the Complete Psychological Works of Sigmund Freud*, translated and edited by James Strachey, volumes 4 and 5. London: Vintage, 2001. First published 1900.

———. *Moses and Monotheism: Three Essays*. In *The Standard Edition of the Complete Psychological Works of Sigmund Freud*, translated and edited by James Strachey, volume 23, 1–137. London: Vintage, 2001. First published 1939.

———. "The Moses of Michelangelo." In *The Standard Edition of the Complete Psychological Works of Sigmund Freud*, translated and edited by James Strachey, volume 13, 209–238. London: Vintage, 2001. First published 1914.

———. "Mourning and Melancholia." In *The Standard Edition of the Complete Psychological Works of Sigmund Freud*, translated and edited by James Strachey, volume 14, 237–260. London: Vintage, 2001. First published 1917.

———. "A Religious Experience." In *The Standard Edition of the Complete Psychological Works of Sigmund Freud*, translated and edited by James Strachey, volume 21, 167–172. London: Vintage, 2001. First published 1928.

———. "The Uncanny." In *The Standard Edition of the Complete Psychological Works of Sigmund Freud*, translated and edited by James Strachey, volume 17, 209–256. London: Vintage, 2001. First published 1919.

Gay, Peter. *Freud: A Life for Our Time*. New York: W. W. Norton & Company, 1988.

———. *A Godless Jew: Freud, Atheism, and the Making of Psychoanalysis*. New Haven, CT: Yale University Press, 1987.

Goble, Frank. *The Third Force: The Psychology of Abraham Maslow*. New York: Grossman Publishers, 1970.

Greenblatt, Stephen. *Hamlet in Purgatory*. Princeton, NJ: Princeton University Press, 2001.

Greven, Philip. *Spare the Rod: The Religious Roots of Punishment and the Psychological Impact of Physical Abuse*. New York: Alfred A. Knopf, 1991.

Hacking, Ian. *Mad Travellers: Reflections on the Reality of Transient Mental Illness*. Charlottesville, VA: The University of Virginia Press.

Hertz, Robert. *Death and the Right Hand*. Translated by Rodney and Claudia Needham. Aberdeen: University Press, 1960.

Homans, Peter. *The Ability to Mourn: Disillusionment and the Social Origins of Psychoanalysis*. Chicago: University of Chicago Press, 1989.

———, editor. *The Dialogue between Theology and Psychology* Chicago: The University of Chicago Press, 1968.

———. *Jung in Context: Modernity and the Making of a Psychology*. Chicago: University of Chicago Press, 1979.

———, editor. *Symbolic Loss: The Ambiguity of Mourning and Memory at Century's End*. Charlottesville and London: University of Virginia Press, 2000.

———. "Symbolic Loss and the Re-creation of Meaning." In *Mourning Religion*, edited by William Parsons, Diane Jonte-Pace, and Susan Henking, 13–43. Charlottesville and London: University of Virginia Press, 2008.

Hustwit, Ronald. *Something about O. K. Bouwsma*. Lanham, MD: University Press of America, 1992.

Jung, C. G. *Memories, Dreams, Reflections*. Rev. ed. Translated by Richard Winston and Clara Winston. New York: Vintage Books, 1965.

Klein, Melanie. "A Contribution to the Psychogenesis of Manic-Depressive States." *International Journal of Psycho-Analysis* 16 (1935) 145–174.

———. "Mourning and Its Relation to Manic-Depressive States." *International Journal of Psycho-Analysis* 21 (1940) 125–153.

Kleinman, Arthur. *Patients and Healers in the Context of Culture: An Exploration of the Borderland between Anthropology, Medicine, and Psychiatry*. Berkeley, CA: University of California Press, 1980.

Kohut, Heinz. *The Search for the Self: Selected Writings of Heinz Kohut*, 1950–1981. Edited by Paul Ornstein. 2 Vols. New York: International Universities Press, 1978.

Kripal, Jeffrey. *The Serpent's Gift: Gnostic Reflections on the Study of Religion*. Chicago: University of Chicago Press, 2007.

Kuyper, Abraham. *Lectures on Calvinism*. Grand Rapids, MI: Wm. B. Eerdmans, 2000.

Lage, Ann. "Beverly Hancock Bouwsma: Observer of Campus and Community Culture, Berkeley Department of History Faculty Wife, 1956–2001." Interview. Berkeley, CA:

The Regents of the University of California, 2008: http://digitalassets.lib.berkeley.edu/roho/ucb/text/bouwsma_beverly.pdf.

———. "William J. Bouwsma: Historian of European Culture in the Early Modern Era, University of California, Berkeley, 1956–1991." Interview. Berkeley, CA: The Regents of the University of California, 2008: http://digitalassets.lib.berkeley.edu/roho/ucb/text/bouwsma_william.pdf.

Malony, H. Newton, editor. *Psychology and Faith: The Christian Experience of Eighteen Psychologists*. Washington, DC: University Press of America, 1978.

Maslow, Abraham. *Religions, Values, and Peak-Experiences*. Columbus, OH: Ohio State University Press, 1964.

McCutcheon, Russell. *Critics not Caretakers: Redescribing the Public Study of Religion*. Albany, NY: SUNY, 2001.

Meier, John. *A Marginal Jew: Rethinking the Historical Jesus*. 2 Vols. New York: Double Day Books, 1991, 1994.

Miller, John. *Jesus at Thirty: A Psychological and Historical Portrait*. Minneapolis, MN: Fortress Press, 1997.

Myers-Shirk, Susan. *Helping the Good Shepherd: Pastoral Counselors in a Psychotherapeutic Culture, 1925–1975*. Baltimore: The Johns Hopkins University Press, 2009.

Novick, Peter. *The Noble Dream: The "Objectivity Question" and the American Historical Profession*. Cambridge: Cambridge University Press, 1988.

Pagels, Elaine. *Adam, Eve, and the Serpent*. New York, Random House, 1988.

Parsons, William. "The Ability to Mourn: Disillusionment and the Social Origins of Psychoanalysis: A Conversation with Peter Homans." *Criterion* 30 (Winter 1999) 2–8.

———. *The Enigma of the Oceanic Feeling: Revisioning the Psychoanalytic Theory of Mysticism*. New York and Oxford: Oxford University Press, 1999.

———. "Mourning and Method in Psychoanalytic Studies of Indian Religions." In *Mourning Religion*, edited by William Parsons, Diane Jonte-Pace, and Susan Henking, 63–80. Charlottesville and London: University of Virginia Press, 2008.

Parsons, William, Diane Jonte-Pace, and Susan Henking. "An Introduction." In *Mourning Religion*, edited by William Parsons, Diane Jonte-Pace, and Susan Henking, 1–9. Charlottesville and London: University of Virginia Press, 2008.

———, editors. *Mourning Religion*. Charlottesville and London: University of Virginia Press, 2008.

Pfister, Oskar. *Christianity and Fear: A Study in History and in the Psychology and Hygiene of Religion*. Translated by W. H. Johnston. London: George Allen and Unwin, 1948.

Power, Mick. *Adieu to God: Why Psychology Leads to Atheism*. West Sussex: Wiley-Blackwell, 2012.

Powlison, David. *The Biblical Counseling Movement: History and Context*. Greensboro, NC: New Growth Press, 2010.

Pruyser, Paul. *Between Belief and Unbelief*. New York: Harper & Row, 1974.

Reber, Arthur. *The Penguin Dictionary of Psychology*. 2nd ed. London: Penguin Books, 1995.

Ritzer, George. *Sociological Theory*. New York: Alfred A. Knopf, 1983.

Schaberg, Jane. *The Illegitimacy of Jesus: A Feminist Theological Interpretation of the Infancy Narratives*. San Francisco: Harper and Row, 1987.

Schultz, William Todd, editor. *Handbook of Psychobiography*. Oxford: Oxford University Press, 2005.

Schweitzer, Albert. *The Quest of the Historical Jesus: A Critical Study of Its Progress from Reimarus to Wrede*. Translated by W. Montgomery. London: A. & C. Black, 1910.

Seligman, Martin. *Flourish: A Visionary New Understanding of Happiness and Well-Being*. New York: Free Press, 2011.

Shiner, Larry. "The Concept of Secularization in Empirical Research." *Journal for the Scientific Study of Religion* 6 (1967) 207–220.

Taylor, Charles. *A Secular Age*. Cambridge, MA: The Belknap Press of Harvard University Press, 2007.

Troeltsch, Ernst. *Protestantism and Progress: A Historical Study of the Relation of Protestantism to the Modern World*. Translated by W. Montgomery. London: Williams and Norgate, 1912.

Turner, Victor. *The Ritual Process: Structure and Anti-structure*. Ithaca, NY: Cornell University Press, 1977.

Van Aarde, Andries. "Social Identity, Status Envy, and Jesus' *Abba*." *Pastoral Psychology* 45 (1997) 451–72.

Van Gennep, Arnold. *The Rites of Passage*. Chicago: University of Chicago Press, 1961.

Weber, Max. *The Protestant Ethic and the Spirit of Capitalism*. Translated by Talcott Parsons. London: G. Allen and Unwin, Ltd., 1930.

Winnicott, D. W. "Transitional Objects and Transitional Phenomena—A Study of the First Not Me Possession." *International Journal of Psycho-Analysis* 34 (1953) 89–97.

Wulff, David. *Psychology of Religion: Classic and Contemporary*. 2nd ed. New York: John Wiley & Sons, Inc., 1997.

Index